C

INTRODUCTION

PART ONE – NORTH

PART TWO—MEXICO AND CENTRAL AMERICA

Contact Bob at:

artinarchitecturestx@hotmail.com

INTRODUCTION

Young men in their twenties are driven to do things that seemed off the wall later in life. What drives us in that period of our life? Whatever it is, it drove me!

The open road called, as it does at a certain age; and I went. Twenty five thousand miles, driving from the Arctic Circle to the bottom of the earth. Across the Straits of Magellan to Ushuaia on Tierra del Fuego, the southernmost place on earth people live. What a year of 'NEAR DEATH' experiences it was. Let me tell you about it. I have written this book in short chapters that bounce along with us in the truck.

In the late 1960's, America and Boulder, Colorado, where I was a student at the University, seemed very tame. The Nation was in a terrible conflict overseas and at home some communities were in an uproar. As many people my age were heading North to Woodstock, I chose to go all the way South. Not meaning to ignore or diminish any of this, I had it pretty easy. When the spring semester ended, a friend offered to pay me to drive him to Alaska in my good old 1962, 4x4, Chevy pickup truck. He had landed a summer job fishing in the Bering Sea, wherever that was. Now, I was born and raised, a New York City guy and before coming to Colorado, two years earlier, I did not even know that there was life west of New Jersey. In spite of this big and little upbringing, I was an adventurer. Young men in their twenties are ready to go on an adventure at the mere mention of it.

The transition from A YOUNG MAN, to A MAN, is sometimes a fast process; this long adventure took me quickly through this Passage to Manhood.

Little did I realize that this little jaunt would take me around the world! Not, however around the world as we usually think of it, but around the world from top to bottom. Twenty five thousand miles, one way, from the Arctic Circle to the bottom of the earth. Like many things in life, it started in a very innocent way. Setting out for the trip to Alaska, we had the usual camping gear. You know, sleeping bag, camp stove, good Colorado boots, and the stuff any young inexperienced guy would think of taking along. We acted like we were going to the moon, and we would be there the rest of our lives. We took way too much stuff, it looked like we were moving. What were we thinking?

It's ironic that when, we next prepared for a truly 'leaving the planet' world trip, we took almost nothing with us. The idea was to deal with things as they came up. Living off the land, whatever it would bring. Let me tell you, it brought plenty of excitement. I also insisted that we have no weapons, that we would use our wits, nerve and naturally our luck to survive. I know we all survived because we did not have any guns with us. We would have been so out gunned any way it would not have mattered.

You will see, in this story, all the danger and adventure of living off the land brings in some of the very remote and dangerous places we stumbled onto.

After the northern country experiences in the Yukon and Alaska, the 'new-old' world of Central and South America over shadowed it. When you read about this huge place, in particular South America and realize how few of us from North America have traveled over its vast wilderness, you will want to go there yourself. It's funny, so little was known about our neighbor to the South, that when I was interviewing guys about coming on the trip with me, one guy said that he would love to go to Latin America, but he did not speak Latin. In the last half century, since we made the trip, access and knowledge of the South has been made easier. The 'Pan American highway' did not exist then. It was tough going and rarely traveled, you faced the hardships as best you could; ALONE!

Young men learn lessons that can serve them for life, especially, when they are faced with consequences that can kill them. I faced many of these 'NEAR DEATH MOMENTS', In the course of those many thousands and thousands of miles. Leaving as a young man and returning as a mature one, served me well in my life. Even before leaving for the trip, I learned a life lesson. I had advertised for people to go on the trip to South America in Denver and Boulder, and lots of guys applied. I narrowed it to six of them and only needed two. I took the six on a three day snow cave cross country trip over the Rockies. I did not look for the best skier or the strongest guy. I looked for one thing. There are three kinds of people in the world. People, who open a canteen of water, drink it and put it away. Then there are the people who take a drink and next offer it to the others. I took the third kind; they offer the canteen to everyone first than lastly take a drink themselves. These are the people you want with you.

One year after returning, I ran for elective office and went on to become the Deputy Mayor of Boulder and to have a successful career in Architecture and building. In the last thirty years I have lived in the Caribbean designing and building many beautiful structures and still have my hand in politics as a newspaper editorial writer and talk show host. A man well trained and lucky can lead a wonderful life. I hope my adventure reminds you of your own special trips or the one's you have always dreamt of taking. Thank you for taking this one with me.

PART ONE – NORTH

NORTH TO ALASKA

Between Colorado and Alaska there is a lot of country. Actually there are two countries, the U.S. and Canada. Traveling north of Colorado, the Rocky Mountains keep you company whenever you look out to the west. It must have been an awesome sight to those first settlers as they trudged along the dirt trails with their oxen teams and covered wagons, heading into these giants. What would you think after the months spent on the Great Plains rolling along on flat ground? How will you ever convince your horses and oxen to climb over these rough mountains? No amount of whipping and coaxing will ever convince these animals to do it. Whatever reluctance the animals might have had, the humans must have had their own fears as well. We thought of this as we, in relative comfort, drove up I-25 to Wyoming, in my good old Chevy pickup truck.

In many parts of the world mountains suddenly shoot up from flat plains. I wonder why. If you were designing things, you think you would put some hilly bumps for a few miles before jumping right into mountains. I guess no one thought of this when the Rockies were pushed up here. This is silly talk, but when you are driving along in straight flat country this is how your mind works. As we crossed the State line of Wyoming, the country opened even more. The wind blows constantly here. It is said that the only thing that breaks the wind here is the barbed wire. I think they are right. In all due respect to Wyoming, it's not the beauty of the front range of Colorado.

This being the first 'border' we crossed I can't help now thinking of how innocent and inexperienced we were. In the following year we and certainly I, would become world travelers well beyond the experience of most people. Border crossings would become one of the unique and sometimes dangerous experiences in the upcoming twenty five thousand mile journey. Right now however, the 'crossing', was only a painted wooden 'Welcome' sign along the road. Here in

Wyoming, the home of the 'wild west', we could see miles and miles, of miles and miles, but few horses. Indeed not much of anything except the barbed wire. The guy who got the barbed wire concession must have made a fortune, if he even got only a few cents a mile. When we reached Cheyenne it was a surprise to feel like we were back in the 1800's Wild West. When you have a boom town that grows up fast and then no one cares to tear it down to change it, time stands still. It somewhat resembles the back lot of Warner Brothers Lot in Hollywood. I guess it's really the other way around, isn't it.

Cheyenne Frontier Days was coming up and we stayed to see it. This parade and rodeo is a trip back to the last century. There is not a man in the entire town without a cowboy hat on his head. It is said that here the only time a man takes his hat off is when the American flag goes by. I have heard some women say they have hung flags over their beds so that their husbands will remove their hats when they go to bed.

These are friendly people, with a big 'Howdy' and a touch of the brim of their hat, when they see you. I thought Denver had a lot of cowboy boots and hats but here hiking boots and a baseball hat is very suspect. We wore ball caps and hiking boots, oops! After the wonderful parade we stayed in town to fully enjoy the 'Wild West' feel of the place. The next day was the 'Big' Rodeo; we hung around for it. I have mentioned to you before that I'm a New York City guy. Did I also mention that I had a horse in the city on the sixth floor? But I did not mention that I worked at a horseback riding stable when I was in college. I had a trick horse and I could jump on from behind, run beside him and spring into the saddle and swing down from the saddle, while at a gallop and pick up a hat on the ground, great stuff for showing off to the girls, and I did.

This Rodeo is huge. There are horses and cowboys and bulls and Indian tribes in full costume everywhere. It's a pageant, done well. I'm sure King Arthur and his Knights could not have put on a better show with their lances and sword fights. The big e v e n t s are the bronco riding and then the biggest, the bull riding and bull dogging. Bulls are a main event in many countries. In Spain, the young Spanish men run down the streets, with red scarfs around their necks with the angry bull herd chasing them. In Mexico they fling red capes around in front of their excited bulls with feats of daring, to the applause of the arena audience. Here i n America's west they do not flash any red capes, they choose instead to sit on them. Well they make every effort to sit on them anyway. Bulls and people have a natural immunity toward each other. Most of us are familiar with our beef on our p l a t e ; for these guys, their beef is under their butts. Any tale of bull riding, from any of us, would be 'bull'. However I do have one true 'bull' story of my own.

Back in New York, in the country where I went to college, I worked my first summer for a riding stable. During that time the owner of the stable also bought and sold horses and tack around the East Coast. I was the kid who went with him to ride the horses in the auctions to make the nags l o o k like they still had some life left in them. One day in Metuchen, New Jersey, at an auction, he bought a long horn steer that had been used for bulldogging, from a small rodeo outfit that was going out of business. When we got the bull back home to the riding stable, all the boys wanted to try bulldogging it. I went first. Out of the shoot ran our new bull, indeed a very experienced bull at all of this. The rest of us were complete novices and especially me. I had seen bulldogging on TV, but never had anyone explain the fine details of how to do it, and more importantly, what NOT to do. I shot out of the gate on my trusty pinto horse and ran up beside the bull as I had seen on TV, I reached down and dropped my arms around his neck behind his horns and let go of the horse. Great first move, only one problem; in the excitement I f o r g o t to take my foot out of the stirrup on the far side of my horse. There we went, the three of us, horse, long horn bull and helpless me, all attached, running at full speed toward the corral fence. Not many choices, I let go of the bull and got dragged around with my foot still in the stirrup by my frightened horse till someone finally jumped down from the corral fence and stopped him. I was 18 and made out of rubber and survived without serious injury, thank you.

Here in Wyoming, they know what they are doing. There is however a lot of air time in the bronco and bull riding. Air time is the space, the air between the rider and the animal. You know you are supposed to keep your behind tight in the saddle. Not possible with these wild creatures. A day at the rodeo was enough so we headed north for more adventure. Montana here we come.

THE CANADIAN BORDER

What a beautiful mountain range the Bitterroots and the Absaroka Range are. They have the majesty of the Rockies but with a greater sense of wilderness. As part of the northern Rocky Mountains they enjoy the protection of the National Park service. Forty and fifty years ago, when we were traveling through it 'clear cutting' was still being practiced. Clear cutting is the logging practice where 'all' the trees are cut in a particular area. This often resulted in tremendous erosion from the lack of trees and their roots to hold on to the soil in the spring runoff. It also looks ugly. We witnessed lots of this clear cutting as we went along. Happily we no longer allow it. The logging industry has also learned the lessons of the past and now practice better managed care.

As we drove through Paradise Valley, and in and out of the town of Livingston, we were pleased to be in so rural a place.

These sun drenched, snowcapped, beauties give you pause. At different times of the day, in the clear mountain sky, the colors change dramatically on the snow and on the giant rock outcroppings of the shear slopes. It is not hard to imagine the historic Indian tribes considering them sacred. We too were moved to sense some higher authority. These great mountains have powerful avalanche runs that mark their faces in strange ways. They also let go of a lot of water in the spring. The Yellowstone River gathers a lot of this water and rushes it North and then South for its long journey to the sea. Water has and is one of the important things people need when setting up a place to live. The Wind River Indian Reservation is located in a beautiful valley with lots of cold running water in the river of the same name. We camped one night here and found it quite enjoyable, though a little windy. As we broke camp the next day, my buddy was at the river washing the dishes when he let out a scream. He had just found a huge moose head with giant antlers attached; this was the perfect ornament for the rock grill on the front of the truck. We envisioned ourselves being seen as great hunters returning from a rough mountain trek. OK; we only found them laying around on a river bank, so what! Speaking of a long journey, we still had a long way to go to get to the Canadian Border, so let's move along.

The Canadian Border is a peaceful place, on both sides, American and Canadian. This crossing is not like the heavy tourist crossing at Niagara Falls for example, but more like a 'Hi, how are you, having a nice day' kind of place. The U.S. Border Guards are happy to see you go, I hope they are just as happy to see us return, and the Canadian guards, who are Mounty dressed, could not be more pleasant. Little did we know how dangerous and dramatic some of the Border crossing would be in Central and South America. This was our first time outside the 'good old USA'. We felt INTERNATIONAL. We felt like we had really left home for the first time. This was a true adventure, beginning right now. Again; how little did we know of what lay ahead, far below, in the Southern World?

We headed north to Banff and Jasper, the Canadian National Parks. Don't think of 'parks' as in the park down the street. These are vast wildernesses, larger than some of our Eastern States. Getting to Banff and Jasper we passed through the small community of Calgary. In all due respect, when you are from New York City, most places look 'small'. Calgary is a very well kept place. I'm sure those living here are proud of their community and we were happy to visit it. Getting from there to Lake Louise in the National Park is easy. The lake is big. On one end of it is a fine tourist lodge, well known for its fantastic views and fine dining. We did not stay there. Instead we found a remote old logging road, put the truck in four wheel drive and headed into the wilderness. As the light started to fade we made camp in a little draw, to keep out the wind. There were mountains all around and many fallen trees. I suppose they were down due to some past severe storms.

There did not seem to have been any recent logging near us. We made a small fire, there was plenty of wood laying all around, and cooked our meal. As usual, our beds consisted of laying branches and twigs on the ground with the space blanket on that, then our sleeping bags. It didn't take long to get it set up. Did I mention that for 'flashlights' we only had two dim kerosene lamps. Simple things that don't give off much light. You could only see about five feet in front of you at best. We climbed into our sleeping bags and then heard the first of the frightening sounds. Rip, tear, crash! What was it? It got completely dark. We didn't think this was the tooth fairy come to grant us a wish! We knew that the area was loaded with wild life, but not the kind of 'wild life' you find at a fraternity party. This is the kind that 'eats you' or at least leaves you looking like you had been eaten.

It crashed again, this time closer to us. When we were in Calgary we met a park ranger who warned us about the unusual number of bear, mostly grizzly bear attacks around Lake Louise. He told us of two women, who just the week before, had been viciously attacked, while sleeping in their tent. They had foolishly brought their food into the tent with them and the Bear smelled it and tore the place and them apart. They luckily survived the attack with treatable injuries, but with scars for life.

The Ranger told us, if confronted by a bear, all you can do is make noise and if he attacks, roll in a ball and play dead. Even the idea of 'playing' dead did not appeal to us. He also emphasized "do not run" they can out run you and you will upset them even more. Oh, that was reassuring. The only thing he left out, was saying your prayers. All this was in our heads as we lay there. The noises continued. They got closer. We got more frightened. We looked at each other like two pieces of bacon

probably look at each other in the frying
pan. Now what? We got up put on our pants
and boots and with our dim flashlights
looked around. I shined my little light where
the sound of tearing was coming from,
about eight feet away and there it was! It
saw me and the light and it stood up. It
looked ten feet tall. No it looked twenty feet
tall. Well, it was a lot bigger than me! A
giant grizzly bear! I yelled to my buddy—
'BEAR', or something. Now at these
'moments of truth' all the training, planning
and forethought, goes out the window.
"Don't run" are you kidding; we flew. Try
stopping yourself and just 'play dead'
when your feet and legs are working just
fine. I guarantee you will run like hell too.
For us the truck was not too far away and in
what seemed like a nanosecond, but was
longer, we were in that truck with a grizzly
outside looking in. He looked at us as if to
say "you are the luckiest guys I haven't
eaten in a long time". That was close, but
luck counts! We were OK. We spent the
night in the truck. The next day we got out
and gathered our stuff and continued north

to the start of the ALCAN Highway at Dawson Creek. British Columbia. There, at mile ONE of the Alcan, everyone signs the billboard, showing the beginning of the road. We left all future generations a slip of paper saying "we were there" how profound! Seemed great at the time. On to the 'highway' then a two lane gravel road with rocks flying at you from semi-trucks passing, one came through the windshield, just missing my head. You don't get stopped; you keep going; or you will never get there! We continued on.

YUKON WILDERNESS-
MOSQUITOES RULE

A lot of open space

THE LAND CALLED---'THE GREAT ALONE'

Mosquitoes own the place. This vast Territory is beautiful in a way we do not see in the lower 48.

The tundra is endless. We hiked over wilderness that had likely not seen many or any humans before. It was early spring. Not summer yet and not the brutal winter this place knows, but that bucolic time between the two seasons. Hiking and camping at this time of the year is easier than in the nightless summer because the ground is still somewhat frozen. The tundra becomes almost a swamp when all the frost leaves the upper part of the ground, the permafrost never leaves. It was early enough in the season that some color was appearing in the plants. How many gorgeous valleys did we stand on the edge of and wondered why no one lived here? The reason no one lives here is not the weather but the flesh eating mosquitoes! Hiking in this environment, the simple things, like taking a pee, become tricky. If you stood still and took it out, the mosquitoes would have a field day. The trick was to do it on the run, and then even if it got a little damp on the front of your pants, at least you were not going to be scratching there all day and all night. There are ten times as many insects here in the Yukon, than in the jungles of South America. I remember reading the Journals of Lewis and Clark, though they were a bit south of here, during the three long years of that epic journey, these tough explorers wrote constantly in their journal of the mosquitoes. For these hardened travelers to so continually mention the agony of these insects is to confirm our agony as well. The expression we and they used every day was "if not for the mosquitoes"!

This part of the world is remote. That's an understatement. There is no road that connects, for two thousand miles to the East. You travel in these valleys along the Yukon River, or you better have a dog sled. We drove north to Dawson. The 'settlement' of Dawson is on the Yukon River. In the late 1800's it was the 'Capitol' of the Yukon Territories. Gold mining was the reason it existed at all and when gold was coming through here, there were even a lot of fancy dressed women around, not now however. The term 'gold digger' did not come from men who 'dug for gold'. The place is frozen in time. Gold fever often ends as rapidly as it begins and here it ended in what seems like a day. I remember climbing into abandoned buildings, that been abandoned fifty years before, still with all the store goods on the shelves. The shelves and the place looks like someone a half century ago, ran in the door and shouted "Get out, the Gold is gone, everyone is leaving". It seems like a ghost wind just blew every person away and left the buildings and all the other things right in place.

It was strange climbing into empty, abandoned buildings on the main street with no one around to care. This town once hosted such famous people as Jack London, where he wrote 'Call of the Wild' and was inspired to form the ideas for other of his great novels. Robert Service was a bank clerk here when he wrote his famous stories like 'The Shooting of Dan McGrew' and 'The cremation of Sam McGee'. Here are a few lines from these poems.

THE SHOOTING OF DAN McGREW—

'A bunch of the boys were whooping it up at the Malamute Saloon,

The kid that handles the music box was hitting a rag time tune;

Back of the bar in a solo game, sat Dangerous Dan McGrew,

And watching his luck was his light-of-love, the lady that's known as Lou.

When out of the night that was fifty below and into the din of the glare,

There stumbled a miner fresh from the creeks, dog dirty and loaded for bear

He looked like a man with a foot in the grave and scarcely the strength of a louse

Yet he tilted a poke of dust on the bar and called for drinks on the house. --------

You should read the whole thing, its great stuff. Also from Robert Service,

THE CREMATION OF SAM McGEE

There are strange things done in the midnight sun, by the men who moil for gold;

The Artic trails have their secret tales, that would make your blood run cold;

The Northern lights have seen queer sights, but the queerest they ever did see,

Was that night on the marge of Lake Lebarge, when I cremated Sam McGee,

Now Sam McGee was from Tennessee where the cotton blooms and blows

Why he left his home in the South to roam round the Pole, God only knows,

He was always cold, but the land of gold seemed to hold him like a spell

Though he'd often say in his humble way, that he'd sooner live in hell

On a Christmas Day we were mushing our way over the DAWSON trail,

Talk of your cold! Through the park's fold it stabbed like a driven nail.

-----'. The rest is a hoot.

I fell in love with these stories and memorized a number of them. I often recited them out loud in the truck as we drove along. My buddy threatened to kill me if I didn't stop. No sense of history. So I kept it down for both of our sakes. Back to Dawson and its place in the gold rush of the 1800's and early 1900's. The strategic location on the mighty Yukon River gave it the attraction to become so central in this remote part of the world, in both finding the gold and getting it out.

At this time of the year, the Yukon River is still frozen. The ONLY road out of here crosses the river. This wild, fast running river is frozen solid for a good part of the year. By this time in spring, all you see is a solid block of ice from the river bank on the one side to the other. The problem is it is not as solid as it looks. Up till a week or so before we arrived it was still safe enough to cross. Oh, I didn't mention that there is no bridge, only the ice road. I asked around about crossing it anyway. I got an equal number of "looks OK to me" as I got "too late, you'll die, if you try". I was told that every year or so they lose a few people who try it when the ice is too weak. They also almost never find the bodies.

Before we get to what happened to us, let me offer one more of Robert Service's poems to help you understand the majesty of this place.

'THE SPELL OF THE YUKON'----

-I've watched the big husky sun wallow in crimson and gold, and grow dim.

Till the moon set the pearly peaks gleaming, and the stars tumbled neck and crop;

And I thought I surely was dreaming with the peace o' the world piled on top.

The summer no sweeter was ever, the sunshiny woods all a thrill,

The grayling a leap in the river, the big horn asleep on the hill.

The strong life that never knows harness; the wild where the caribou call,

The freshness, the freedom, the farness— Oh God how I stuck on it all-----'

You too can feel the draw of it all. This vast wilderness 'CALLED' many a man and destroyed a great number of them along the way. To the west of here lay the Chilkoot Pass. From the sea, where many miners came ashore, they had to climb this shear trail, which took days and days of hauling their gear up to the top. It was so severe that many of the mules they brought along could not take it and died on the trail. In fact it became such a problem with miners driving dying animals up the trail that the Canadian Mounted Police stood at the top of the pass and shot any animals that had bones sticking out of their sides. In the photos available of this horrific time you can see hundreds of bearded miners climbing over the carcasses of the dead animals. What a driving force Gold is.

Sorry for the diversion, but I thought you might enjoy these poems. I think I was about to tell you what happened on the icy Yukon River, that we wanted to cross. The tracks on the ice of the trucks that had made it during winter were still visible. The question was is that the best place to try it. We were still being advised NOT to do it. The locals, including the Mounties, advised against it. I was determined to try. Now trying did NOT include a SECOND CHANCE. If you are wrong, there is no turning back. There is only one direction THRU, DOWN and DEATH.I debated not taking a chance but that did not appeal! So the only consideration was where to chance it. The rutted path the earlier trucks had taken seemed to me now to be the weakest part. I figured all those heavy trucks had likely cracked the ice below. Not that I really knew, but it seemed a good guess. Now I looked for a fresh way to cross. The river here is about as wide as the Hudson River is in my native New York City. I never thought about driving across it, but I'm planning to drive across this one.

I figured it might be best to go slow across. Then I thought it might be safer to go fast. I got opinions on both sides of the debate. Go fast—go slow; I don't know! We found a spot with solid ice right up to the shore line and it looked like as good a place to go for it as any. A number of locals gathered on the bank to witness our ride. It's hard to know if they were praying for you to make it or hoping for you to lose it.

I calculated the ice would be harder in the early morning, before the sun got on it. There we were, the good old red Chevy truck, my buddy and me, facing what could be our last moments. The local folks around on the river bank were silent. I put the truck in four wheel drive and on a wing and a prayer floored it and went as fast as I could out on the ice. The cracking ice below frightened the hell out of us and it felt like at any moment the great river was going to open its mouth and swallow us whole. I don't know how fast we were going but it did not seem fast enough. I remember staring bug eyed at the opposite shore and it didn't seem to be getting any closer. The thunder of the cracking ice got louder and my heart reached my mouth. Then suddenly splash, bump and we were across. Firm land never seemed so firm ever b e f o r e . The folks on the Dawson side gave us a cheer and we waved our thanks. I'm sure we thanked everything we could think of thanking, and off we went to the

Alaskan border.

Rush Hour in the Wilds

AS NORTH AS IT GETS FOR US

Alaska had not been a state for very long before we got there. It was not even ten years old when we arrived. Clearly the childhood of statehood did not reflect on its climate or the snows that are older than time! Crossing back into 'new American' Alaska, was easy. At this time of the year we were one of the only vehicles coming from the Yukon via the river crossing. In fact, the border guards wanted to know how we did it. I showed them the rosary beads and said we floated over on them. One laughed, the other guy didn't get it. It was a joke. Oh well, not everyone gets a joke. We got back on the Alcan headed for Anchorage. Anchorage in those days, like any city, was loaded with lawyers and bars. If you have a lot of the one, you get a lot of the other, they had plenty of both.

Again I must apologize to Anchorage, as you know, I come from New York and was not impressed with the place. We didn't visit any lawyers but we did visit a few bars.

After the wilderness of the Yukon I will admit that having a hot shower, fifty cents at a local motel, was great. My trusted traveling buddy stayed here after we found his boat. He was excited to get on board and head for the unknown of the Bering Sea, and the life of a fisherman. Well, the life of a fisherman for one summer. I headed north for Fairbanks.

It's easy driving here in 'America', the roads are paved and the signs make sense. I say this now, after the thousands and thousands of miles in Central and South America where there often is no road and signage consists of asking enough locals about where the next place is. To get more than a 50-50 opinion, you must ask an odd number of people, for if you ask an even number you will likely get half saying one way and the other half saying the other way. We always tried to ask three, five or seven people.

My plan had been to work in construction for the summer in or around Fairbanks. I had heard that there was plenty of building going on there and I could make good money. I mentioned in the 'Introduction' that I was a skilled carpenter, and in Boulder I was working my way through the University 'RAISING A HAMMER FOR PAY' that is to say, working as a carpenter. I had all my tools with me and I knew how to use them. I drove around Fairbanks looking for something under construction, but could find nothing. I then spotted a house being framed and stopped to see about work. I found the foreman, showed him my tools, told him how experienced I was and that I was ready to go. He looked at me and said "kid, we get ten young guys every day like you looking for work; there is NONE, sorry, and he went back to what he was doing. That was disappointing! At this point I had spent all my money. I think I had about seven dollars left in my pocket and half a tank of gas in the truck. All I had left to eat was a cheese sandwich, a can of soda, and a few Ritz crackers. This is not going to work. I decided to find the State Employment

Office, where, as a good citizen of the USA, they would save me and find some work for me, so that I did not starve. The office was close by and when I parked the truck and walked around the corner, to my amazement, there was a line of other hungry guys a mile long. Well, it seemed like a mile long. You will not believe this, but as we stood there in line, a Government unemployment worker came along the line of men and handed each of us a sheet of paper. It read "Thank you for coming to Alaska, Sorry but there is NO WORK; we hope you have sufficient money to get home. GOOD LUCK!" It should have included 'come see us when you have lots of money to spend, not when you think you will make some here'. This was not good.

Someone on line, said he had heard of work in the town of Circle, about one hundred miles north, just below the Arctic Circle. It was worth a try and I had just enough gas to make it. Circle Alaska turned out to be bust. No work there either and lots of guys looking as well. I was broke, so I decided to sell the truck. The good old Chevy 4x4, three quarter ton, long bed pickup must be worth a fortune up here. Wrong! The only used car dealer in town told me he gets lots of these trucks offered to him every week. So many people drive up here from the states and can't or don't want to drive back that trucks are a dime a dozen. Yikes! Now what? I drove a little way up the road and took out my National Geographic map. This was one of those that show each state and also a map of the world. I looked at it and saw that I was as far north in the world as you could go on a road that connected to the rest of the world south. It fascinated me that it was possible to drive from here to the bottom of the EARTH. Around the World, North to South. I had never heard of anyone doing it, I assumed others had, but surely if I did it, I would be in a very rare club. Giant decisions some times are made on the spur of the moment. I decided to do it!

To celebrate my decision, I ate my last cheese sandwich. Naturally, driving to the bottom of the earth was easy to say; but something else to do. With nearly an empty tank of gas left and almost no money, I could not even get out of Alaska to say nothing of getting to Ushuaia, across the Straits of Magellan, on Tierra del Fuego, twenty five thousand miles away. Before despair could set in, luck struck. Two guys, loaded down with camping gear, were walking and hitch hiking right past me. I called them over and they told me they had been camping along the rivers up here for a week and had finally gotten eaten by mosquitoes to such a degree that they were going to fly home to Seattle, Washington. They had planned the trip to last three weeks and still had two weeks of vacation left. I made a deal to drive them down, so that they could see all the wonderful things between here and Seattle and give them a worthwhile vacation. They cashed in their airplane tickets and gave me the money, which was enough for gas and food for the trip south.

About two weeks later I dropped them at home in Seattle and went to look for work. I was again out of money. Immediately I found a big building being framed and talked the foreman into giving me an hour to show how much I knew about carpentry. He hired me after only ten minutes of work. The next day he asked me if I would like to go up in the mountains and frame some fourteen houses they had contracted to build near Mount Baker. I did and spent the summer in the beautiful little town of Granit Falls. I took a contract to do the framing on a fixed price and made a lot of money working twelve and fifteen hour days.

September arrived, it started raining every day. I drew my last pay and headed back to school in Boulder.

PART TWO – MEXICO AND CENTRAL AMERICA

LEAVING THE HOME COUNTRY

Not like mom's house

Not Whole Foods

Leaving Colorado; heading south. Heading 'south' would be a term I'd use over and over for a long time to come. The road south through New Mexico is easygoing. It's not mountainous, mostly dry country with a few interesting things to see. It's pretty flat and boring for many miles. You can't imagine why anyone would live here, but there they are now and then walking along the road and in little houses set way off in the distance. After leaving the majestic mountainous beauty of Colorado this is; well this is, the absence of beauty. Let me admit to you now that as the months passed on this long adventure that I would learn to see the beauty of where I was at any moment. We had our National Geographic map out and it was clear the border was not far off. Except for the time in English speaking Canada, all of us had spent our entire lives in our own country. Even this strange desert countryside felt like "home".

It popped up all of a sudden from around a curve. I recognized the familiar Red, White and Blue of course, but just beyond it was a strange one. We knew what it was and naturally had seen pictures of it before, however it was still a shock. God, you can be so dumb and innocent when you are young. This, being the sixties, the Mexican Government had decided that "hippies" were a grave threat to their country and banned anyone with a beard from crossing the border. I had grown a huge, and I thought magnificent red beard. Back in Boulder, girls thought it was a beauty as well, but not in Mexico. So it was gone and a clean shaven, for the first and last time in fifty years since, I looked like a clean cut guy. None of us had ever seen so many guards, gates and guns in one place before. Leaving your country in those days was pretty easy. Passports, a look in the eye, and a wish in English of "good Luck". A few hundred feet beyond the "good Luck wish" was a different world. I should explain that I was the "Spanish speaker" of our group. My Spanish consisted of four years of high school Spanish and absolutely no use of it since then. Thinking a good smile would do as much as poor high school Spanish I said "Oley" and handed over the passports and the Carnet de Passage documents which allowed the truck to enter. Stamp, stamp, stamp and we were on our way. We felt like we had just broken out of prison or gotten away with something. We were so innocent crossing the Mexican border with all the guards and guns, it felt like escaping from the Nazis to us.

We drove along at a good clip, on reasonable roads. The old '62 Chevy 4x4 pickup seemed happy as we were; now we were going to really be starting the "GREAT" adventure.

Nuevo Lerado was not exactly a garden spot, but it did have some local restaurants. Actually, everything was local in those days, no Mc Donald's, and we were hungry. I noticed that there were two kinds of restaurants, those with bright fluorescent lights that lit the place up as if it were a sports arena and the ones with dim "mood" lighting. Stateside dim mood lighting was preferred. Here, the brightly lit ones were showing that they were clean and had no cockroaches. We chose a bright one. We had been told that the food in Mexico is OK and the people are friendly and the trips to the bathroom are frequent. All this is true. On the intersection of the pavement we were on and a dirt lane, we found a place to eat, parked and went in. It was morning so we sat and decided to order breakfast. Well the other three guys looked to me to order. Thinking I'll show off my Spanish for the first time, I ordered "Helados Fritos". The waiter looked at me in a strange way, so I said it again more slowly. "Helados" and sat back with a certain international satisfaction of being bilingual. He came out of the kitchen with the cook and had me repeat the order. I, realizing I had not told him how many I wanted I said "dos". They went off mumbling something in Spanish when a customer, who had overheard my Spanish, told me I had just ordered two fried ice creams and had probably meant to say "huevos" eggs, well it was close. In a foreign land you must begin somewhere.

The country side was desolate but friendly. Horses, horse carts, donkeys, donkey carts and plenty of walkers. It was interesting but strange; there were so few cars and so m a n y animals that at times we would not have been surprised to see a Wells Fargo Stage coach with John Wayne coming along. We drove on to Mexico City. A bustling city with a larger population than my home town of New York City, just more spread out. Thank goodness I learned to drive in New York because I had some chance of keeping up with them here. It's like driving in NYC, except they have abandoned all the traffic laws. Up to this time, we had been camping alongside the road or in open country. No camping beside the road here, this is a city. As a born and raised big city person, I knew there were two possibilities for finding a safe place to be. Find one of your relatives and stay with them or because we did not know a soul; ask a cop. We didn't know a soul, so that was out.

Now where is a cop when you need one! After driving around a while we saw two police cars and some military vehicles by a stadium. Over we went, my Spanish was a little better and I asked where we could safely park and camp for a night or two. In big cities, parking your car and leaving it is always risky. In Mexico City, it can be deadly as well. They understood my improved Spanish and gleefully lead us around the empty stadium to a desolate spot and looking at us like a shark looks at a school of little fishes, said the equivalent of "don't worry, park here" and grinned. To a city boy, it didn't feel right. While I was maneuvering the Chevy, I noticed that the Army trucks were moving in a way to block the exit. All my instincts kicked in, I put the truck in four wheel drive and floored it. We bulldozed across the playing field and a newly planted garden, leaving a trail of dust and mud flying. For some lucky reason, they didn't chase us or shoot. I now wonder whether they were good guys after all, I'll never know that or if I did the right thing,

After a few more days of visiting the historic spots and seeing the great museums, we continued south into the country side. Life on the road is easier in the open spaces of nature.

Small Pueblas and family farms come and go like eye blinks. They start to blend in your head as one. My Spanish was coming back. At least my vocabulary was. How I made sentences was suspect at best, but I always got an understanding and often a laugh. Telling a young Senorita that her hair is blue when you meant to say her eyes were blue, provides lots of attention, but produces little success.

We continued southeast to the historic old port city of Vera Cruz. Before the Panama Canal was built at the beginning of the twentieth century, this was the port where most goods and people crossed from Atlantic to Pacific. There had been a small narrow gage railroad connecting the two coasts but it was a slow and expensive process unloading ships, then onto small rail cars and then again loading them on the Pacific ships. During those hundreds of years this port was a busy place. Now it was a sleepy place. It did have the remnants of some beautiful architecture and I love historic architecture. I must say it was worth the extra effort to get here and see it all. After two days, we again headed south.

Two way road

KEEPING YOUR FEET ON THE GROUND—THAT'S – BULL

I had heard of the beautiful historic small city of Mazatlán for years and wanted to see it. The Colonial Spanish architecture of the city is legend for those seeking a glimpse of the past. It's easy to find, the road was OK getting there and we had no problems with "bandits". It is something of a tourist town, though few tourists were there when we arrived. On our second day in town, I heard some English being spoken by some "gringos" and went over to say hello. They were going to a bull fight, put on for the locals and the few gringos who were interested. I was eager and off we went.

Now in Mexico, bull fighting, like in Spain, is a sport. In the U.S. we do not think fighting animals is acceptable, they do not agree. Not only do they feel it is acceptable they often hold these events on Sunday after church. At the entrance of the ancient stone arena you had a choice. No, not smoking or non-smoking, but spitting or non-spitting. I chose NON. This turned out to be the section with the respectable class of locals dressed to the nines. I guess, dressed as I was, they looked at me and thought I should be in the spitting section. The action began as I had seen it in the movies with the Picadors and their beautiful Paso Fino horses, followed by the cape carrying handsome young Matadors. Perhaps because it was Sunday, or the price of beef was low, or for the sensibilities of the gringos, they did not kill the bulls that day, only pricked them a little. It was still an exciting event.

After a few bulls got pricked and the capes had been flung around for the benefit and cheers of the audience, a bugle sounded and an announcement in English was made. Any gringos who would like to try fighting the bulls can come on down to the lower part of the arena. In a flash I was out of my seat and down under the arena. About five guys showed up. Now remember this is not an OSHA approved event, nor is it a helmeted, padded football game, but a primitive blood sport. They told us in "Spanglish" that it was a simple matter to fight the bulls; perhaps they meant "survive" fighting the bulls. Our instructor, a very well made man of great stature told us what to expect. He had an assistant push out a wheeled homemade canvas bull's head with the necessary attached horns. Each of us got first hand tries with our assigned red capes to let the pushed bull dummy "run" under our cape. Oh, this is easy. Actually it is easy, if at the moment of truth you can remember to do it right. Naturally none of us had any experience with this before. Let me explain. As we know the guy with the cape, the Matador, waves it, the red cape, around till the bull sees it and decides, in his own time, to charge it; or more correctly to charge you. We all tried it several times. Then he told us once more the MOST important thing is, wave the cape and at the last moment when the bull is close, STEP away from behind the cape. He will run straight; you move aside. Whatever you do, DO NOT

MOVE THE CAPE AND STAND RIGHT THERE, move you not the cape. We practiced and thought we had it. I did anyway. We drew straws to see who would go first, I won. They gave us some fancy outfits to wear and with the trumpets blowing, the Picadors and the horses in front, we entered the bull fighting ring.

Like Christians being led to the slaughter, we paraded around. The women threw flowers and horns sounded, it felt great. Having "won" the toss I stood alone in the arena while my brave comrades ran for cover behind the barricades. Silence fell upon the crowd as the gates to the bull pen opened and out rushed my opponent. It was mortifying and relieving at the same time. This was no great big bull but a "BULL- ETT". You think I was scared, he was scared to death. I was surrounded with creatures of my own kind, he was with no one he knew. Now as much as there was relief for me, he only got more upset.

Even being half the size of a full grown one, there was a lot of animal there. After checking out the place, he found me. I guess there is some instinct that says to a bull, even a bull-ett, this guy should not be here with me. He came running! In ordinary daily activities, we tend to do things without much thought. We cross dangerous streets by looking both ways, we drive our potentially deadly cars comfortably, we do many things on a daily basis that could cause us much harm, and we do them with a lot of practice and get good at them. Bull fighting was new to me and here I was stepping off the curb, blind.

I mentioned earlier that at the "moment of truth", any moment of truth, you can't know what you will do. You can practice one thing time and again but at that moment, anything goes. You would be amazed at the speed of one of these creatures when they know what they are after. As our eyes drew closer together I MADE THE GREAT MISTAKE, I swung the cape and stood there. Wham! I went flying.

He hit me so squarely in the gut that I flew completely over his back into a warm, freshly deposited pile, he had just dropped. The picadors came running, diverting him and carrying me out. Thank God I was y o u n g and nothing was damaged except for my pride. However I cannot say I lived to fight another day. That was it for me. I hung up my cap and cape for good. But I did it!

Doing all the 'it's' was what this trip was about.

It's Bull

A SAFE BATH & A BAD MEAL

You get pretty sticky and sweaty in the jungle. We had been driving and hiking around these parts for some time now and we needed a bath. Our hotel on wheels, the Chevy pickup truck, was not the Ritz. The camper shell had everything except for water, sewer, and lights. In fact, as I may have mentioned earlier, it had a sheet of plywood and a thin foam pad over that with sleeping bags spread around. In other words, no shower. Here in the jungle, there was plenty of running water, it ran in murky streams. We had seen many of these, not inviting, streams as we traveled about but never went in any of them. Traveling as we were we heard lots of stories of giant snakes. I hate snakes, and as far as I was concerned all snakes are one size or another of an Anaconda.

On this very hot and humid day, anything wet was needed. I spotted a stream just ahead on this soggy trail and it looked to inviting to pass up. In an instant our clothes were off and in we went. It was wonderful. As luck would have it there was more than a muddy stream but there was also a deep pool out a ways. We were like little boys at the swimming hole, laughing and splashing, except this was not safe Kansas.

A few days earlier we were warned about a tribe of natives not friendly to outsiders. Los Indios de los Colorados. They were described as headhunters. You know, the one's with the shrunken heads hanging around their waist. Sure, I thought, this is one of those stories you hear all the time to scare the gringos. We were no pansies and afraid of nothing; I thought. The swim was great, we splashed and fooled around. Then one of the guys looked up and saw we had company. On the muddy bank, standing over our clothes, were a bunch of fierce looking Indians covered in red mud. Los Indio's de los Colorados, the red Indians we had been warned about.

Picture yourself in this position; you're naked, up to your neck in a jungle pond, with all your stuff at the feet of these savage looking people. People covered in red mud with spears, no shields. Even if you thought they were smiling it would be no relief, you always smile before a good meal. What to do? Swim away, no chance. Be friendly, it had always worked before, OK try it. Having no idea if they spoke Spanish I said as firmly and friendly as my naked self could say; "we are travelers". I really wanted to say we will be disappearing in a second if you let us, but I didn't. The biggest guy, with the most feathers, came forward and put out his hand to pull me up the bank. I thought is this Hansel and Gretel with the witch feeling my hand to see how much meat was on it? It's crazy the things that go through your mind when faced with a complete unknown. It turned out, as before, they spoke a little Spanish, at least the big guy did; he was the chief.

While they seemed quite comfortable to be almost naked, we did not. We got dressed as they watched us with great curiosity. Now humans, even those as different as we were, have a certain understanding of who is who. I guess the chief saw that I was the "chief" of our little tribe of white guys and treated me with great respect; thank God! The Chief and I grunted and nodded and said a few things, then he invited us over to the tribe's camp or settlement or basically where they hung out. Home to them was not what we would consider "home". Here in the jungle you don't need four walls, keeping the rain off is the extent of what you need. As we walked into the village two things struck me right off. There was a fire pit with glowing hot coals and large, semi domesticated, rats running around. These capybaras are the largest rats in existence, about the size of a mid-size dog. Word had spread that the Chief was having another "chief" and his little tribe over for dinner. So some of the women ran after two of these "rats", hit them over the head, and threw them in the fire. No, they didn't skin them or gut them or remove the hair, they just threw them in the fire to cook whole. The Indians in many parts of the world make something resembling beer. It's definitely not Coors but as close as you could get in this remote village. As the women prepared the meal, we men sat around on huge elephant ear leaves in a clearing and drank, the beer stuff. It was potent. As we were to discover with other remote people we were to meet, children are much too curious to be frightened for long. Soon we were surrounded by lots of kids staring at us, perhaps never having seen a white man before. Now and then I looked up to see how the women were doing with dinner. They were all fussing around the fire and talking in a language I could not understand. Suddenly the chief signaled for us to eat. I guess there was some proper etiquette in the tribe, so he motioned for me to sit next to him. You know, "chief to chief".

With great ceremony he waved his hand as the women approached with dinner served on big leaves. As his honored guest he and I were both served first. With a big smile the senior woman gave each of us the two

snarling rat's heads, eyeballs and all. It's
great being chief, isn't it? My host looked at
me and could tell I didn't know how to
approach the head. With the big smile of a
good host, he sucked out the eyeballs and
then waited for me to follow suit. I cannot
tell you what eyeballs taste like. I must have
turned off my taste buds and just
swallowed, both of them. Pleased, he then
showed me how to suck out the brains.
Yummy, yummy, the best rat's brains I have
ever eaten.

While I was dining on these delicacies, my
"tribe" was eating some unrecognizable
parts of the animals. If they had not been so
frightened of our hosts they would have
been in hysterics at the look on my face as
I stared eyeball to eyeball at my meal. It
was getting late and like all dinner dates we
said good night and much to our surprise
and relief they led us back to the main trail
where we found our way back to the truck.
The next day we were off once again ready
for the next adventure that might come our
way.

WHEN THE SHOOTING STARTS

When the shooting starts---duck! Now you don't need training for this, it comes naturally. By the time we got to the Honduras border we had seen plenty of guns, from pistols to submachine guns. Ever where you go in Mexico and here in Central America uniforms and guns are on display. The Guardia National are armed to the teeth. The bandits are as well, but have the good sense to keep their weapons under their shirts. At each border crossing, there seems to be a desire to show off the countries hardware. Some of these crossings are better protected then East Berlin ever was. I don't know if it was because we were U.S. Americans or too young to worry about but we never were hassled. There were quite a few times that we had machine guns pointed right at us with sixteen year olds holding the trigger. At each border crossing, my Spanish got better and better so that I could more easily answer their questions.

Question number one: any guns? No

Señor! Any drugs? No Señor. Any women? No Señor! Solomentry Vuestros y nada mass. Just us four bearded wonders, nothing else. Stamp, stamp, stamp; passé.

It almost started to feel routine. We were to learn not much is routine in Central and South America for long. About five hundred feet from the border, the shooting started. You know you don't at first recognize shooting when you are not used to it. I guess it took a few seconds for one of the guys to yell, they are shooting at us. I can't remember if I said "holy sh—"in English or Spanish but the reaction was the same, get out and get down. When you're scared, time is measured differently than when you're calm. It seemed like it took us forever to get under the truck, it probably took a Nano second. Now what? Where are they? Who is shooting? Are we safe? Is everyone OK? How do we get out of here? The four bearded ones had no idea what to do. As we calmed down a bit it became clear that whoever was shooting was not shooting directly at us. Or if they were they were lousy shots because none of the bullets hit our hard to miss big red truck. Shots were flying all over the place so we crawled out from under the truck to get an idea of what was going on. Like you see in the movies, uniformed military solders were hiding behind buildings, parked cars, and anything they could find and squeezing the bullets out of their machine guns like crazy. The guys on our side of the border were shooting across to the other side of the border, which was no problem for us. The problem was that the other side of the border had enthusiastic shooters as well a n d they were shooting at us. My guess is that neither side had a lot of target practice before this eruption. I'm sure there was not a bird left in the sky or in a tree as the lead flew wildly. I will say they all looked pretty serious about this business and no one seemed to be in charge. Sort of every man for himself. Even I realized this is no way to have a war. We need leadership!

Both sides must have had the same ammo budget because they stopped shooting at about the same time. In a gun battle you don't want to be the first guy to stand up thinking they are out of ammunition. It could be a trap. So we all stayed where we were waiting for the next move. As is the case with great excitement, someone suddenly has to pee and decides he can't hold it any longer. He is the brave one or perhaps dumb one who just runs for it. In our case one of our bearded wonders made it to a wall and all was well.

Coming from the U.S. we didn't know the rules for a border war. There was no one in our upbringing who told us what to do or what to expect when being shot at. Is there some kind of understanding that these border guards have? Is it that, we each shoot off a few rounds then go back to normal? Is the deal we wait till we all have to take a leak then quit? What's it all about? I guess they can hold it for a long time because the shooting went on for a few days. It turned out the "war" was over a soccer match that one side or the other thought was not fairly won. In a very excitable culture, a border war is to be expected at any time. Just when you don't expect it, an Inquisition happens.

When a truce was declared, or they finally ran out of bullets, or all the birds were killed, or they forgot what they were mad about, or whatever, it was a treat to get back in the old truck and head off again. Here in Central America the land mass is relatively narrow. The roads are very passable, actually better than the Yukon and the gravel, rock flying, unpaved Alcan Highway. With the mountains to the east, the road stays to the west. The countryside is very beautiful. The people are friendly and the roadside eateries, which serve the local truck drivers, have a life all their own. It's hard to call them truck stops, as we think of our highway gigantic one's, but they serve the same purpose. With one exception they also contain the second families of some of these more romantically driven drivers.

Sitting and talking with some of these guys at their bar and food shanties gives you a full picture of how life is lived here. Enthusiasm is a driving force in this culture. There is enthusiasm for work, when they feel like doing it, there's enthusiasm for food and drink and most of all for love. Judging by the number of kids running around here, they must be good at it as well.

The idea of this trip, besides the big one of from top to bottom of the earth, were little ones, like meeting local people and viewing their lives. The big red truck was one of the door openers that I had not planned on. In small pueblos, villages, when we pulled in with it, with its powerful winch on the front and the big rock screen across the grill and the huge tires, front and rear, painted real fire engine red, we looked like the military, some branch of it at least. In this part of the world looking like the military is not a bad thing, you get respect. In some villages we were looked at as scientists on a mission. In any event we did not look like tourists down for the weekend. So on we went, looking as important as we could, given the dirt and tatter of our clothes.

LAGO de NICARAGUA – CREATING THE WORLD'S BIGGEST SHORTCUT

The long dead volcano

that created the Panama Canal

Crossing from the Atlantic to the Pacific oceans has interested Europeans for hundreds of years. If you look at a map of Central America it is not hard to imagine that the three 'narrow' spots could be dug out and ships could pass through. This has been in the dream of engineers since the early eighteen hundreds. However no one got their shovels out for a long time because on paper it looked good but in reality it was all but impossible. Canal digging has been popular for many centuries in Europe, the Middle East and even in the U.S. with the completion of the Erie Canal. It takes a stable government and lots of money which depends on that stable government. Central America always lacked political stability, even when it had the 'doable' routes. Asking investors to put up the vast amounts of money to dig a canal when at any time the corruption and fragility of the sitting government could erupt in revolution or unfriendliness made the dreams go away. Just ask France about their attempt to dig the first Panama Canal.

When we drove into Nicaragua I wanted to see the great Lake in the center of the country. I had read some things about it and it fascinated me. This is one of the largest fresh water lakes in the world. In the U.S., we have some mighty big ones as well. They are considered 'Great' by us. Here the locals are very proud of their 'great' lake as well. This big lake has some unusual features that even ours does not have. Here, the lake, which as I mentioned is fresh water, has sharks. I was amazed to find this out when a local fisherman told me so. He told me as I was about to go for a swim in the lake. Thank you for the warning! These bull sharks swim into the lake from the sea by making their way up a small river much like salmon do. It takes them about a week to make the transition and they seem quite satisfied with themselves at being able to do it. However in the lake they continue to act just like sharks, ouch!

You and I were talking about creating a canal between the two oceans. When we were in Mexico we drove to Vera Cruz, on the Gulf of Mexico. Here in 1519 Cortes came ashore and liked the place, though it was a little hot and humid, but he still laid claim for Spain. The United Nations was not in existence yet, so no one complained. This was only the second Spanish settlement on the mainland 'New World'. The Spanish, whatever you think of them, formed here, the first city council in the new world. They formed a small bit of democracy before anyone else thought of it here. The early Spanish did not have time or money for a canal, or even a road across the Isthmus; it was left to future generations. In 1853 the Gadsden Purchase by the USA provided for a plank road and then a railroad between the oceans. It worked pretty well if you were not in a hurry. Many of the '49ers' heading to the California gold rush passed over this route. Engineers proposed a canal to replace the land route but it proved too risky due in part to the Mexican Revolution that was fermenting at the beginning of the twentieth century.

The next possible place was Lago Nicaragua. If you look at a map you too would make this conclusion. The distance from coast to coast is a little greater than In Mexico but there is this huge lake in the middle to reduce the digging. The lake is very deep, 85 feet deep across much of it and seems to keep itself full all the time. At the turn of the century a good, seemingly stable dictatorship was in place and these 'Boys' liked the idea of lots of U.S. money coming their way. The US Congress was determined to create a water passage across Central America by hook or by crook. At the same time the Nicaragua Canal was being promoted, a second canal in Panama was being resurrected. The French Government sold its rights to what it had worked on for a few disastrous years, to the USA. Both canals had powerful interests pushing them. Both projects made some engineering sense. The enormous desire to stop having to sail around the bottom of South America and all the dangers and expense it entailed, drove both plans. The

Nicaragua plan had people like Cornelius Vanderbilt pushing it. One of Vanderbilt's companies already had a stagecoach running from Lago Nicaragua to the Pacific coast and he wanted to put the canal through. Panama had its proponent's as well. Not the least of whom was Teddy Roosevelt. Mighty Men with mighty big ideas. The problem was we needed only one canal and the U.S. Government had to pay for it, which meant Congress. There was a lot of money involved, so you can imagine the lobbying that went on in the halls of Congress.

The debate lasted through a complete session of Congress. Every Congressman had piles of maps and engineering studies galore on both proposals. Lobbyists met with anyone who would stand still long enough to have the maps rolled out in front of them. If CNN had existed then it would have had twenty four hour coverage of the goings on. As the decision deadline drew near it looked like the Lago Nicaragua Canal would get Congressional approval. It was argued that it was closer to the U.S. and therefore could have troops sent there faster if there was trouble. In addition the friendly Nicaraguan Government said 'come-on down'. Panama on the other hand was part of suspicious Columbia and a long way away.

The day of the final vote arrived and it looked like it was in the bag for the Vanderbilt gang of Nicaragua, when out of the blue an opposing Congressman passed around a blown up copy of a Nicaraguan postage stamp. The official government stamp showed the two volcanoes in the center of Lago Nicaragua spewing volcanic smoke. Here he said is why we should not build this canal across this dangerous lake, it could blow at any minute! The truth be known the two volcanoes had been extinct for millions of years; but who knew? Congress voted it down and subsequently approved the Panama Canal.

In life the smallest things can make a big difference, they can float or in this case sink your ship. For me standing and looking at this pristine lake I was personally happy for the misinformation all those years ago, so that I could swim in the lake. Each of us took turns watching for sharks while the others enjoyed a cool swim. Life is good!

THE ONLY GAP

Looking at the maps, it's clear, that Central America is a much contested place. Now that we have made it to its bottom, Panama, with all the revolutions and heavily guarded borders, it's a mess, politically.

It occurred to me one day, as we crossed the border from Costa Rica to here in Panama, that if you put together all the "national" maps, the one's that each country displays as their territory, Central America would be twice as big. For example the map proudly displayed at the military border crossing for Costa Rica shows it as a country with pieces of both its neighbors to the north and to the south. The neighbors of course do not agree and on their maps claim, in print anyway, territory from their neighbors. As a visitor it's humorous, as a country, it can mean war.

Panama is a strange place. It is really two places tucked in a barbell looking configuration.

There is the Central American part north of the canal, then the huge jungle south of it, the start of South America. You could even say there is the third part, the mechanical and social belt around its stomach, the canal zone. Funny to see the stars and stripes flying in so remote a place. We are here in the dirty, busy harbor of Panama City. In contrast to the sleepy little city of Colon' on the Caribbean side of the canal, this is a bustling port. Speaking of Colon', named for Christabel Colon, or as we call him Columbus, there are some hundred or so tiny islands off the coast called the San Blas Islands. There the natives of this mostly uninhabited chain, make very interesting hand stitched little fabric things called "molas". They are very proud of their handiwork and when you go through the trouble of getting there by small boat, [we left the truck in Colon], they are very happy to see you and show off their wares. We bought some of these colorful 'molas', I don't know what I'll do with mine but I'm sure I'm not coming back here again, so now or never.

Back in Panama City we are trying to get a boat to get around the Darien Gap. I'm a determined guy. I was determined to make this entire trip by land but someone put the densest jungle in the world right in the way, the Darien Gap. Before deciding it was impenetrable, we tried driving into it. It would be more accurate to say that it tried to eat us, truck and all, after only a few thousand yards of travel. It is so dense that when you looked behind, where you had just driven, the jungle had already closed in to the degree that you could not see your own tracks. The year before we got there National Geographic tried to get through with helicopter drops of supplies, a bunch of Land Rovers and very experienced explorers. They only got half way after several months of slugging, and gave up. Having no helicopters or big money to pay for equipment, our little gang of young explorers gave up also, only a lot sooner than they did.

By now, my Spanish was pretty good, but my traveling companions were struggling with only a few poorly pronounced words. One day in Panama City one of the guys went to the open air market to get some provisions. He decided he needed some eggs. Not knowing the words for eggs he looked about but didn't see any. Pointing works as well as words, but you have to see them first in order to point. After a while he went up to a fish vendor and with great theatrical expression said " Senior donde' esta los 'pluck, pluck, pluck, he turned reaching under his behind as if taking out an egg' The local fish seller looked on in utter amazement as did the others nearby. While Laughter did lead to getting the eggs and made some new friends. Inquiring at the docks and at the market I heard that there was a small tramp freighter planning to sail out in the Pacific around the Darien to a jungle port in Columbia. She was leaving in a few days, if there were no more problems with the government. She was called, in English, "Good Hope", it turned out she should have been named "No Hope". I got down to the docks and found her tied to the old pier but resting on the bottom. Not an encouraging sight. There was lots of activity around her and I was told that indeed she was going to sail soon, on the full tide, when she would be floating again. The Good Hope was as much rust as she was steel but I was assured that the trip around the Darien would be no problem, Senior, only two days maybe three at the most, "no Problemo Señor". You know, now that I think about it, the real name of the ship should have been "solamente problemas" {only problems}. With the tide out and resting on the bottom she leaned away from the dock and was about ten or twelve feet higher than the dock. Now I should mention that this was not a very big vessel. She was about 150 feet in length and a beam of about 16 feet, slim and long, built to take the rough seas of the Pacific. When she was built was anyone's guess, certainly not recently.

After looking her over from the dock, I thought "why not" and proceeded to find the Captain. A rough looking sailor was yelling instructions to another rough looking sailor on board about not scraping off too much rust, for it was the only thing holding the ship together; I said hello, in Spanish of course. This guy was not exactly the friendliest person on earth, just a look and a grunt. I asked if he were the Captain, he answered with the equivalent of "are you kidding, that SOB is not around". I asked if he was the first mate, a look and a scowl; 'Si'. The red truck was right there so I pointed to it and asked if we could pay for passage to Columbia. He looked at me and the boys and the truck and shook his head in a manner that says "are you as dumb as you look," then said "porsupuesto"{of course} and sized us up to see how much he could get. We agreed on a price, I forget now what it was, but it was affordable. There was one problem, [actually the first of many problems], how to get the heavy truck up to the ship's deck. The old rust bucket had a winch but when I inspected it I didn't think it could have safely lifted me, to say nothing of the truck and all its gear. Luckily I spotted a huge pile of wooden pallets lying about and with the help of my companions we built a long ramp up to the deck height. No sooner than the great bridge was complete then the tide started coming in and the ship rose. We couldn't keep up with the higher and higher deck so we decided to wait for the ebbing tide to get the ship to our ramp height. What geniuses we were, surely you agree. Let Mohammed come to the mountain, instead of the mountain coming to Mohammed.

The hours passed, we waited. Little by little down she came and settled in the mud. We didn't have long before she would start up again so we worked fast. Now pallets make for a lumpy and bumpy road so we found some old plywood to put a better roadway on top of them. With the truck in four wheel drive and the truck winch hooked to the ship's rail, up we went, at least up I went. A huge crowd had gathered around us to witness this great engineering feat, with I believe, the hope that it would fall into the sea. Like inwardly wishing, but not outwardly wishing, that there is a car crash during a stock car race, our audience hoped for our success but secretly wished for our failure. I was at the wheel of the truck, one of the guys climbed up the ship's mast to get some good pictures of the event and the other two stood and hoped and prayed that I made it.

You can imagine my relief when the truck and I landed across the ship's deck. I wasn't sure I'd make it. Relief from one problem always seems to lead to another problem. In our excitement to build the ramp and get up it, we forgot to measure the beam {width} of the ship's deck where we would land. At that point the deck was narrower than the truck with the tailgate open which was our only way into the little sleeping camper and all our stuff. Picture the pickup bumper to bumper touching the ship's rails and the tail gate hanging out over the side with the sea below. No going back now!

We settled on board and engineered a way to get into the back of the truck. Now we waited and waited for the Captain to come onboard.

TIME WITH THOR HEYERDAHL

I thought I was on an adventure. I guess if you get around enough you will meet the dandiest people. Perhaps that's what Heyerdahl thought of me. That would be giving myself too much credit.

One day in Panama City, before finding the 'Good Hope' to carry us around the Darien Gap, I was in a small bar getting a beer to cool off. I sat down on a bar stool next to a rugged looking Nordic guy. After getting my first gulp to cool down, he turned to me and admired my red beard. I thought this was nice and he appeared ok, so I took it as a simple compliment. He himself looked like he didn't work behind a desk either. His English was halting with that wonderful Viking way of pronouncing things. We started up a conversation and the inevitable "what are you doing here" came up. I went first and told him of my goal of getting from the Arctic top of the world, to the near Antarctic, almost bottom of the world. He asked about problems we had had along the way and I told him about some of the shooting adventures and the funny times as well. After giving me time to blow my horn, he said who he was. I felt like a kid trying to impress a grownup with school yard stories. Yikes; this was a true adventurer, I was only a kid on a lark. Here was the real thing; here was Thor Heyerdahl of Kon Tiki.

I knew all about Kon Tiki, the unbelievable 1947 float trip that seemed like suicide when they left and almost was as they went along. Kon Tiki was a balsa log raft constructed in Peru, to demonstrate that early man could have used the trade winds and currents to cross thousands of miles of open ocean from the Americas to the Polynesian Islands. He and his crew of misfits and true sailors did the seemingly impossible; they sailed four thousand three hundred miles in one hundred and one days, and made it without any loss of life. Though no shortage of excitement. His leadership had been an inspiration for me to make my trip and I told him so. He was flattered. He said he had many people tell him that they were inspired by his voyage, but he seldom ever met anyone, who so inspired, ventured forth on their own trip of discovery. My head was bigger than it deserved to be. By the way, he had only one beer himself, so I took what he said as true. Why not?

When you are as engaged at flattering each other, as we were, one beer is not enough, so we had more. Then he told me of his next adventure. He told me about the 'Ra11'. Heyerdahl was not the kind of man who sits on his laurels and just collects the good stuff from what he has already done. He does the next 'impossible' thing, after almost dying on the previous impossible thing; the' Ra'1. The first Ra was built at the foot of the Pyramids from reeds similar to the ones ancient Egyptians used for their boats. It sailed well for longer than anyone expected and almost made it, but at sea, after a line was mistakenly cut it started to list then sink in the open ocean. Luckily a passing sail boat saved them and everyone survived. At the time we met he was in his mid-fifties and I was in my twenties. He seemed like an old guy to me then. It was getting late, but still with plenty of day light and he invited me to see it. Thor Heyerdahl inviting little me to come out to see this reed thing he was planning to once again cross the Atlantic Ocean on. As I mentioned, this was his second attempt to do this. The reed craft was anchored in a cove near the docks and we rowed out to it. I can tell you, as someone who has spent many years, since this time living and sailing the open ocean on sail boats; this was no ocean liner. This made a life boat seem like a safer bet on which to cross the Atlantic. We tied up next to it and stepped aboard. It was a wet vessel with the sea splashing over the reeds. I imagined being way out there in the Atlantic, with nothing but you, the crew and water everywhere, including where you were sitting. He asked me if I wanted to go along on the voyage. Not knowing if he was serious, I declined. I jokingly told him my goal was only to sail around the Darien not the Atlantic and besides there was no room for the red truck on board and the truck and I were inseparable. We rowed back and said good bye. I will never forget that afternoon. These things happen only once in a life time and only when you have something to offer the other person.

I met up with my boys, told them what had just happened and with whom, and they too were impressed. We then got back to solving our own problems and left the Atlantic Ocean adventure to my new 'friend'; Thor Heyerdahl.

AT SEA ON GOOD HOPE

She was no yacht

If you have ever been on a luxury cruise ship with all its comforts, think of what the exact opposite might be while being onboard The Good Hope. This was it. Forget about a swimming pool, we didn't have any running water, or for that matter any water at all. As for bathrooms, more properly "heads", there were none that worked. We were told, "Use the rail". Ok, we're tough young guys, we can make do but we forgot one important thing: food. In all the excitement of getting on board the ship and its engineering and construction requirements of the ramp building, we forgot to get anything to eat for the journey out to sea. So you say just go get some, you're at the pier where there are vendors nearby. Trouble was we had already cleared out with Customs and could not leave the ship. We were in no one's country, legally, men without a country, in between everywhere and nowhere.

Panama in those days was not a very enlightened place. If it wasn't a third world country, it was more like, two and five eights. On the dock, which was a constant coming and going of heavily armed Guardia National troops, we kept a constant lookout for "our" Captain. A day and a night passed, still no sign of him and no info from the "first" mate; what an unpleasant guy he was. At least he could get on and off the ship but he refused to get us any food. What little food we had was running low. Except that we didn't have on chains, we were prisoners, unable to do anything except wait.

On the night of the third day, suddenly the whole dock lit up with military vehicles, sirens screaming and troops all around, with machine guns at the ready. In the midst of all the confusion came a big shiny army jeep with flags flying and soldiers snapping to attention. In it, a general or someone with more gold braids on his shoulders and cap than the Queen of Sheba. The jeep moved slowly and as it came close we saw four men walking behind it, chained to the back of the General's jeep. By this time in our long journey, from the Arctic to here we were accustomed to seeing hard and rough things but this was over the top. One of the crew, standing next to me on the deck said "mira, el Cap-e-tan", the Captain was one of the men chained to the jeep. A soldier came over to the chained men and unlocked them. With an armed guard the "Captain" and the other three were thrown on board the ship. It happened, perhaps on purpose, that the tide was in so the ship was afloat. With no warning the dock lines were cast off by the solders and we floated out into the dark harbor. The Captain, who was badly beaten and could barely stand, ordered the anchor dropped so that the engines could get started. He then ordered the First mate to chain the three men who were put on board with him and throw them in the hold. The three were chained up and two were thrown in one of the main holds, while the other one was put into the anchor chain locker, not a nice place. Then he, the Captain, dropped into his bunk and was not seen again for some time.

What is going on here we asked. Well it turned out that when the "Good Hope" sailed into Panama, she had on board these three guys who were convicted criminals and were illegally entering the country. In Columbia these criminals had been forcibly put on the ship by the police to be returned to Panama where they were wanted. It turned out that they were not wanted in Panama. Not wanted in the sense that Panama wanted to be rid of them. Somehow, word of their arrival had reached the authorities in Panama that they were on board so that when the Good Hope tied up to the dock the prisoners, along with the Captain were arrested, and "interviewed" at police headquarters.

The "interview" consisted of beatings, and no sleep and other methods of persuasion to convince the captain to take them back to Columbia. Now our captain knew that if he returned with them to Columbia he would get the same treatment from the cops there. They didn't want these characters back either.

When dawn broke the crew had gotten the engines started. They had worked on them all night. You never saw such a grease covered bunch of men in your life. It looked as if each one had dived head first into a bucket of grease and then rubbed himself over the moving parts of the engine and drive shaft. The crew was made up of a mix of men from all over South America. There seemed to be about a dozen or so, it was hard to tell because some were around very rarely. During the days spent tied to the dock we had gotten to know some of them. From them we heard interesting stories of different places in South America. Coming from different countries they filled in some picture of what we're going to encounter when we got there; [if we got there]. No sign of the Captain but the First mate looked like he knew what he was doing and raised anchor and steamed out of the harbor, bye, bye Central America.

Leaving a harbor is always a thrill. One, you get a different view of the port from the sea and there is some "fond" farewell you feel.

There is also, in this case, a "glad to be out of here" feeling. The old rust bucket seemed to be moving along pretty well. Back on the dock, I had some fear that it would never run, but here we were chugging right along. The grease monkeys even had smiles on their dirty faces.

The Pacific Ocean is not passive. Whoever named it so played a longtime joke on the world: pacific means passive; wrong! When we hit the rolling waves of the open ocean, the Good Hope pitched and yawed like a cork. She did not have sufficient ballast, due to not having any cargo except for us, the red truck and the three prisoners below. During the first hours of this bouncing around we became concerned that the truck would bounce off the deck into the sea. Luckily the ship had plenty of deck chain on board, some of which had been used to chain up the three 'guests' below deck. We tied the truck down real well with some extra chains and were then able to rest ourselves.

We sailed due west, straight out to sea.
After a while the coast disappeared from
view and even birds no longer visited us.
We were out there. The sun dipped into the
clear western horizon. Since this voyage, I
have spent several years living on board my
ketch rigged sail boat, sailing the ocean
seas. The sound of the boat making
progress, way, through the water is a
comforting sound. Sometime, just before
dawn, after steaming all night, the engines
stopped. Dead silence. The only sound was
the slap of the waves on the hull. The
eastern sky began to lighten and with it our
Captain appeared. He was bandaged up
from his encounter with the Panama Police
but walking ok and carrying a rifle. He waved
the rifle around as he shouted out orders in
an angry voice. My hope was that it was an
angry voice, not a frightened one. We came
to find out later that they never had been
out of sight of land before. When they
sailed back and forth between Panama and
Columbia, they kept the coast in sight. The
ship did not have a working compass and no

other navigation equipment on board. These were a bunch of land watching 'BUS DRIVERS' who happened to be driving a ship now lost at sea. As I mentioned earlier we had almost no food with us and virtually no drinking water. In our haste to leave Panama, even the crew had not gotten provisions. It would not have been so bad if we had done the usual three day trip along the coast but now we were lost out in the deep blue Ocean.

I have to give them credit; they worked on those engines night and day as we drifted along. When you are adrift you see different things in the sea than when you are moving under power. The ocean creatures come along side as if to ask "why aren't you moving?" Looking over the rail at their wet and deep watery world you realize you do not want to join them in it. The next morning, we awoke to the sudden sound of the engines coming to life. Well one engine anyway. Our fearless Captain, still with his rifle in his hand, took the helm and had enough sense to head due east into the rising sun, toward land. With only one engine and it barley running, we chugged along. The next morning, a wonderful sound was heard, a crew member yelling Tierra, "land Ho", it's the same wonderful sound in Spanish and English. As we drew closer to the coast, the Captain recognized where we were and altered course south to reach Columbia. The difference in landscape from Central America and the huge size of South America becomes visible immediately. From a couple of miles out at sea the mountains and the hills look empty. Every now and then a village could be spotted but it was clear there were a lot fewer people here than north of the canal, in Central America.

At dusk, we were near the harbor entrance but the captain didn't want to enter the narrow and dangerous channel in the dark. So in rolling seas we laid off, till first light. At dawn we entered. This little, rough jungle port was mostly for banana transport. There was a small, narrow gage rail road that brought the bananas to the ships. At the time there were no ships in the harbor, except for one lying on her side on the shore; it didn't look much worse than our noble vessel.

We steamed toward the dock. Suddenly a speed boat with sirens blaring and loaded with armed Guardia National troops came along side and yelled to the Captain to stop and not to proceed to the dock. They said to drop anchor where we were and for the Captain to come with them ashore. Ahh- oh! Naturally we did as we were told. With the anchor down and things quiet, hunger pangs set in. We had not eaten almost anything for days and we and the crew were starving. This little harbor luckily was full of fisherman and banana cutters in their canoes. Along with the crew, we hailed some of these guys and got lots of bananas and fruit and some fresh fish; it was good.

Just before sunset the captain returned and said that in the morning we could go to the dock and unload. What happy words these were. As the sun rose we raised anchor and got over to the dock and tied up. On the dock were the "friendly" {yea} armed police to greet us. Sort of the 'welcome wagon' of Columbia. The meanest looking one of them all, yelled up, in Spanish, to the crew and I guess us as well; "hi boys, I hear you brought us three gifts back from Panama." We had forgotten all about the three prisoners in the holds. A crewmember went over and opened the main hatch and dragged out the two who were in there. They had not eaten anything since leaving Panama and were nearly dead. He then opened the small forward anchor locker and dragged out the other one. He was dead. The Guards came on board to see for themselves and with no ceremony and no prayers, threw his body overboard and carried off the other two. The sharks and the fishes in the harbor had a great meal that day but we did not pay any more attention to it and tried only to save our own skin.

Two things were now a problem. First was clearing customs and the other was that this time the deck of the ship was lower than the dock. I went off to see about clearing in. On the far side of the dock was the government clearing house. They were always easy to spot with flags flying and sleepy armed guards all around. It looked more like a New York City candy store hang out, than a military post. Inside, were the usual sleepy officials, never anxious to be disturbed. Having gone through this a number of times in other countries, I knew what they wanted. All our passports and papers, as well as the truck's papers were in order. A disgruntled look in the eye from the customs agent, and stamp, stamp, stamp, and then back to sleep he went.

I hurried back to the ship and with the same clever engineering, only this time in reverse, got the truck up on the dock and we were off to see this huge place called South America.

PART THREE – SOUTH AMERICA

IT'S HOT IN
THE JUNGLE!

The author with an Elephant Ear Umbrella

YOU ARE NEVER ALONE—THE INSECTS, SPIDERS AND SNAKES ARE THERE TOO

I cannot say it often enough "I hate snakes"! Since my teenage close encounter, I have had a distain for them. Growing up in New York City we didn't have snakes, but we had other frightening things instead. In the jungles and all the tropical and sub-tropical parts of Central and South America are loaded with all kinds of creatures, big and small, dangerous and not so dangerous. Camping, as we were, with sleeping bags on the ground, and only a 'space blanket' to lay under them for a little protection, it was a risky business.

The jungle floor is a moving carpet. Sometimes a flying one as well. I remember many incidents, one in particular, where we were scared out of our wits when suddenly a snake {remember there are all Anaconda of different sizes as far as I'm concerned] came slithering out from under my space blanket after I sat down on it. This snake was big enough to eat an elephant, well OK, he was big and he scared the hell out of us. That incident brought back memories of why I hate them so.

When I was fourteen, I was camping with my favorite older cousin in upstate New York, where he lived. We had set up camp on a beautiful ridge overlooking the Hudson River. A gorgeous spot. It was early fall and the air was crisp. During the night it got quite cold and it took a while to warm up the sleeping bag after getting in to it. When I woke in the morning, my cousin was already up restarting the camp fire. I yelled to him that there was a snake in the sleeping bag with me. He, being four years older, said "every boy at fourteen wakes up with a stiff snake in the morning". I yelled not that kind of snake but a real one. It took a while to convince him that I was not kidding. Then he thought, what am I supposed to do, I'm not reaching in there and getting bit by it. Finally I convinced him to get a stick and unzip the sleeping bag from the outside because the snake was on the zippier side of the bag. When he opened it, out crawled the snake, after having had a nice warm place to sleep for the night, it then disappeared into the bush. Since then "I have hated snakes".

During this long, long trip we were to encounter so many different creatures it is hard to remember them all. I do remember some interesting moments, at the time it seemed like hours, with huge insects attacking. We often joked that the mosquitoes were so large here that they didn't bite you right off; instead they carried you back to their nest to work on you there at their leisure. Some of the bugs, like the kissing bug, is not really very romantic.

Tarantulas scare the hell out of you with their speed and determination to get you. Lizards and spiders and the rest keep you aware of your surroundings at all times. The colorful designs on some of their shells or wings or feathers gave the early inhabitants, the Mayan and the Inca, ideas for some of the designs on their pottery and wall art.

In Alaska and the Yukon, there are ten times more insects than there are in the jungles of Central and South America, hard to believe, but true. Naturally in the tropics, the insects are a lot bigger and more dangerous than up north. One day in Ecuador we were driving in a swamp like area with the windows down, it was hot and humid, and suddenly a giant frog jumped into the cab. Panic struck as this huge green and blue thing leapt all over us. I almost lost control of the truck and before I could even hit the brakes, it decided we were not good company and hopped out.
This didn't happen every day but it happened often. One time we had been hiking in a rough area of marsh and swamp when one of the guys stepped on a 'tree branch' which sprang alive and bit him on his hiking boot, luckily doing no harm. So many of these places are all but complete living things. Something that at home would be a dead tree branch is not that here.

As we got more accustomed to all that lived around us we became more cautious about what joined us in the truck and our camp sites. We never put our boots on without shaking them out first. You would be amazed at what creatures love the aroma of dirty smelly boots. We shook out our sleeping bags before getting in and we opened the doors of the truck and chased out any snakes or other varmints that decided to go for a ride. With this caution and some dumb luck none of us ever got seriously injured or caught any of the many diseases that kill so many in this part of the world.

Speaking of sickness, I was only sick one day. Before getting some of the visas we needed, we were required to get a series of injections at the hospital in Boulder. The most painful was a series of injections in the stomach for malaria. It was frightening to see that big needle coming toward your stomach and it took three injections over a period of several days, ouch! I caught a flu bug when we were crossing the Equator in

Ecuador, where the road runs over a several day slug up to about nine thousand feet. And there, on the peak, is a stone monument marking the equator. Rising behind it was the twenty one thousand foot peak of Mt. Chimborazo. We had on our down jackets, it was cold. Imagine crossing the equator with winter coats on, this country never ceases to amaze me. I guess this sudden temperature change or something gave me a whooping twenty four hour virus. That and the mountain sickness we all felt in the high Alto Plano that was the extent of our disability. It's just as well because the only medicine we had consisted of band aids, aspirin and a bottle of rum.

THE LONGEST DESERT

A lot of sand and only a few of us

Finally someone legally crossing
our border

We thought we knew what dry was before seeing this. The unbelievable variety of this huge continent continues to surprise and amaze us. Driving in the great Peruvian desert is all consuming. I mean it totally occupies your vision, your sense of smell, your awareness of other things and your sense of having left your familiar planet. I had read about this place before getting here but like many things we read about when you get there you are not prepared for what you find.

I'm sure if you are born in one of the world's great deserts it looks normal and quite natural, as I guess you expect all the rest of the world to look like. For most of us trees and grass or even those of us from big cities, concrete and occasionally trees with occasional central parks are the norm. This is another planet. In the movies, the desert scenes show huge sand dunes and of course camel trains crossing them. South America does not have camel trains and few sand dunes, but it does have lots and lots of sand. To tell you how your mind works, at any moment if Laurence of Arabia came riding toward us we would not be surprised. Here, however, he would be out of work, for there are no Arab tribes to unite.

Having recently been in the jungle where keeping the road, more accurately, the "trail" open is a matter of filling in the potholes and leveling off the mud ruts, which they do a few times a year, this makes it pretty smooth. In-between those times it is rough going, thank goodness for our four wheel drive and winch. With memories of the mud paths we had encountered in the jungles, this is easy going. With no natural barriers to consider, the road is fairly straight. We were following the tracks of previous vehicles, even though we had not seen any for some time. The government has had the good sense to put in markers every now and then so when the trail disappears in a sand storm you can find your way. These simple posts are similar to the ones used in northern U.S. States to mark rural roads in deep snow. The sand was so solidly packed that I had the truck all the way up to twenty miles an hour. I didn't dare go any faster for fear of the inevitable deep pot hole. Twenty feels like we are flying anyway.

The desert road gets very close to the Pacific at points. We are on a ridge line about a hundred feet above the surf. Off on the horizon, on the shore, we spot, what from this distance, looks like a person. You must yourself imagine a completely desolate place for as far as you can see and imagine spotting someone, alone, in this inhospitable place. What are they doing here! Are they friendly! Is it a trap of some kind? If anything happened to you here no one would ever know or even find your remains.   I am sure even Inspector Clousou would be lost. We drove on to see what or who it was. As we got closer our 'person' rose up, opened its wings and flew off. It was a giant condor, one the largest birds in the world. For a moment we felt like we were in a prehistoric world, luckily no dinosaurs, just this great prehistoric creature souring overhead.

Along we went till near night fall. It is too
dangerous to drive at night. One, you can't
see much, there are more chances of attack
from bandits, who can see your headlights
coming, and you are tired from the days
adventures. Camping in the desert is easy
compared to the jungle. As I have
mentioned, the sand is pretty solid so
shifting into four wheel drive you can go
almost anywhere across it.

The fear of bandits was constant. That is to
say we were always aware that we would
be targets. A nice big juicy truck to steal
would have been the prize of a lifetime for
any self-respecting thief here about. Being
unarmed, we had no way to hold off an
attack. Running was our only means of
defense. Because we wanted to have a nice
fire to cook by and for warmth, it gets
pretty cold in the desert at night, we
needed to be far off the road for protection
and so we could see well in advance any
lights coming our way. Remember, it was
pitch black here at night, no lights or

humans anywhere.

Sleeping in the desert sand is ok. With your sleeping bag and the space blanket underneath to keep creatures and dampness out, you could groove yourself into a comfortable spot and get a good night's sleep. Before turning in, a cooked meal became the best ceremony of the day. One of the guys had become a fairly decent camp fire cook; I would not go so far as say 'chef.' This was never a dining experience, only an 'eating' one. Water was always a concern and we never wasted any. It turns out that sand washes dishes very well. After you have licked your plate clean, [never waste food], rubbing them around in the sand does a dishwasher's job very well, it might even pass the health inspector's test.

Dawn comes fast and bright when there is nothing to shade it. The dark fingers of the night unfolded to allow in the morning light. With a quick breakfast, off we went. We needed four wheel drive to get back to the road, then we could shift out. On the hard packed sand two wheel drive was enough. This saved gas and made for a smoother ride. We carried about fifty five gallons of gas with us. The truck's gas tanks held twenty gallons, the additional gas tank I had added in Boulder held another ten gallons and then we had several five gallon military gas cans strapped to the sides of the truck. All in all we could get between the infrequent 'gas stations' we found along the way. It turned out that the road, often the only road, was used by the military of the different countries as their means of getting to trouble spots, so they too had to have fuel stored along the route.

By midday the sun got pretty hot and the wind started to blow hard. It started to look like the Sahara, with sand rolling across the desert. It got hard to see anything, so we pulled off the road and waited for better visibility. The sand storm created some spectacular funnel clouds, mini tornados that channel the sand into tubes of terror.

Fortunately none came too close but you never know; you know! It only lasted an hour or so and ended as fast as it had started. All was quiet. Only one problem, the road disappeared. Like a snow storm up north, all is covered. The difference here was that there were no snow covered parked cars to indicate where the road might be. Before the storm it was a vast wilderness with a ribbon of ruts to punctuate it, now nothing, except miles and miles of miles and miles. Even before the sand storm we would encounter a fork in the 'road'. A number of times we came to a divide, where one set of tire tracks went one way and another of the same size went off in another. In places, not as remote as this, we would wait and ask passing Indians which way to the place we were heading. The first time we did this we asked six different people and got three saying left and three saying right. After that we always asked an odd number of folks so at least we got a majority opinion. Often the map showed only one route, a lot of good it was.

We drove in the direction I thought was best, after a while we came over a slight rise, and then to our amazement we saw the 'highway department' at work clearing the road. Don't get me wrong, we were happy to see anyone, but this was the biggest joke of government at 'work' that you could imagine in your life. As far as you could see there was sand. There was nothing but sand. In the middle of this vast wilderness of desert was one guy with a shovel digging out the drifts on the road. If he lived to be one hundred and worked seven days a week, he could not clear the miles of dunes on the road. But he was trying his best. The sand flying off his shovel made a huge ark over his head in one of those images you could not stage. We stopped to talk to him and to admire his efforts. He said this was his work and the local government paid him per mile cleared. He had a big family and was very proud of his work and all his kids were proud of him as well. He told us we were not far from a settlement and there we could get out of the sun and have a rest. We went on and soon found his village. It was a nice break.

As you can imagine getting out of the hot sun and having some new people around was a treat. We stayed a short while, but before we got to comfortable, I decided it was time to continue on. Into the truck we climbed and off we went. The surrounding country is barren desert. Nothing to see except sand and way off in the far eastern distance, mountain ranges. Picture a barren plain where you could drive in any direction that you pleased with no sign of life anywhere. Then you come over a small rise and there, up ahead, small stones on the desert floor leading to a little shack in the middle of nowhere with a flag flying and a border crossing barrier across the desolate landscape. Remember that funny scene in 'Blazing Saddles' when the bad guys "we don't need no stinking badges" come riding across the desert, in the middle of nowhere, to Rock Ridge only to find a toll gate in front of them. Well this was it. With a little turn of the steering wheel we could have just driven right around this countries border. We did not. As we came up to it a sleeping border guard in his underwear got startled, he woke up and in a fright ran into the shack, closed the door and a few minutes later came out fully dressed in his best army uniform. I expect we were the first 'border crossers' who bothered to cross legally in a long time. Once again, stamp, stamp, stamp; [he was very proud of his stamps], and we were off to find the border crossing to Bolivia, wherever it was hiding.

"Anyone know where Bolivia is?"
The not well-traveled Pan-American Highway
(those are our tracks)

LOST DURING THE MOON LANDING

While they were landing on the moon,
we were lost on Earth

Is it possible that almost 50 years have passed since we landed on the moon? Well naturally you and I didn't land on the moon ourselves, we gave the job to Neil Armstrong and Buzz Aldrin. They did a fine job of getting there and home again safely after making history. Buzz Aldrin, the last survivor of that great event, asked people [of a certain age] to write to him about where they were on that momentous day. May I share my story with you?

I WAS LOST HIGH IN THE ANDIES. We were above 10,000 feet, off the National Geographic maps and in a twelfth century world, really really lost. Back to the day of the moon landing. Having been out of touch with the outside world for some time, we had no idea that the landing was taking place. While you were living in the later part of the twentieth century we were traveling, in the early twelfth century, amongst very remote people. How we got off the National Geographic maps I don't know, we were driving across the high Alto Plano when suddenly one of the guys turned on the radio, which we had not bothered to try for ages and the overseas US military broadcast of the landing came on. At that same moment we came over a rise and there was a remote stone Indian village. As had happened before when we encountered these sparse villages, the people at first hid themselves. In short order the children were too curious and came out, followed by the men then finally the women. As these Quechua Indians gathered around the truck, I jumped out to greet them. It was one of those rare days when the moon is still visible in the sky during the day. I proceeded to translate in Spanish what was happening on the moon. Yes, I told them we were, this very moment, WALKING ON THE MOON, which I pointed to for full effect. Now these people were living in stone huts never having seen a truck before to say nothing of a tall red haired man with a big red beard. They understood what I was saying, knew what the moon was, they looked at it all the time but WE WERE WALKING ON IT? What planet did I come from? I guess not wanting to hurt our feelings they all just nodded their heads but the look of disbelief was in their eyes. I realized I was a time traveler for them and no way could I skip so many centuries in a single breath. It is an interesting thing to be a visitor from the future as I was to find out in the upcoming months on this fantastic journey down the incredible remote world of South America. Over the next many months, of this near one year trip, we were attacked by armed bandits, by Indians, held at machine gun point many times by both bandits and Guardia Nationals and survived by luck and quick wit. Thank you Neil and Buzz for that "ONE SMALL STEP'.

While our native friends were recovering from the moon story, one of our guys happened to pull out a Frisbee we had in the truck and flung it to one of the other guys. Now this was not a thing known in this part of the world, so our new friends were amazed. Children the world over cannot contain their enthusiasm for long.

We passed it to one of them. In an instant he passed it to one of his little friends and in minutes a big round robin of new Frisbee players was born.

Thinking this was the day to continue to introduce the twentieth century to our village friends, I pulled out the tape recorder and asked the kids to say or sing something. Again it did not take them long to sing one of their local songs, which I recorded. Then to their amazement I played it back to them. They studied the tiny recorder to figure out how they all fit in there while still being standing outside it. If you think the children were astonished; you should have seen the adults. I'm sure I could have started a religion around the recorder, they were so mystified by it. The next Mayan culture, naturally making myself King.

I hesitated about bringing out the real magic, between the moon landing shock and the fun Frisbee, along with the tape recorder mystery, our new friends had a lot to absorb. I could not help myself. I dug in the truck's glove box and got it. In those days they were, by today's standards, pretty primitive devices. We had almost never used it before and I had to look it over for a few minutes before I remembered how it worked. It was a little complicated and I wanted it to work the first time for full effect. If you are going to be a new God in town, you want your magic to look good, right off. It keeps the believers coming back.

I was ready. I lined up the head men of the village with the chief in the center, for full effect and proper position. Snap, shoo, click and the little Polaroid Instant camera captured them all. These Polaroid's did not give you the picture right away. First a muddy piece of paper rolled out of the bottom of the camera, and then you held the paper by the edges for a few minutes as it developed. I had the men gather around me as I held the paper. Then slowly but surely the image appeared. I don't think 'astonishment' is too big a word to explain the look on their faces. You must realize these people had never seen a picture of themselves before. In this remote part of the world even if they had seen cameras pointed at them before, they did not know what it did. There are no drug stores to get film developed here, to say the least. So even if someone had taken their picture before, which is unlikely, but possible, they would have had no idea of what was happening. This time they did.

Now you and I know what we look like. We have had mirrors in our houses since childhood and stood in front of them getting ready for school every day. No school or mirrors here. What was amazing was that the chief and others did not recognize themselves but recognized the guy standing beside them, then realized that must be 'me' next to him. What time travelers we were! What fun it was. That night they had a great fiesta for us and we ate a lot of something unrecognizable, but tasty.

ATTACKED BY INDIANS

It had been a long time since we got the truck above fifteen miles an hour. It wasn't a problem with the truck; the problem was with the bad dirt roads, if you even want to call some of them roads. As we climbed out of Lima, on the way to Lake Titicaca, the elevation changed rapidly. Lima, which is not far above sea level, had plenty of air for us and the truck engine to breath, but as the elevation increases the air got pretty thin. There was only one road heading east. The way to Lake Titicaca and then Cusco was a well-traveled route for the first few miles. It was a heavy truck road used to bring goods and more important people out of the Capital, Lima and up into the Alto Plano's many small villages. It was easy to get directions and even the National Geographic map showed it correctly. We found it and joined a caravan of several two ton open body Lorries slowly moving up the switchback road. These heavily loaded trucks moved in second gear, at about fifteen miles an hour, just as we did. The whine of our straight six cylinder engine had become all too familiar to us; hour after hour we lumbered on. What a good truck this is I often thought. I always wanted to write to General Motors and tell them of my love for this tough Chevy pickup. It is said that on a sled dog team there is only one dog with a decent view; the front one. The same can be said in a truck caravan on dusty roads. We were in the rear; the view consisted of the dust of the heavy Lorrie ahead of us and the same for him with the guy ahead of him and so on. The consequence is, I'm not really sure what the countryside looks like outside of Lima, or outside the truck's dirty windshield. You could not see a thing.

The first miles passed with some of the big trucks peeling off on little dirt paths leading to small settlements that are not even on the maps. The distance to Lake Titicaca is a few days travel. Without the other trucks, I thought this must be interesting landscape with the giant Andes Mountains beginning to rise up all around. As yet, the dust keeps the view from sight. As we climbed higher the other trucks started to disappear. By the second day we were almost alone. That night we drove off the road and set up camp, out on the flat plains, to get some sleep and get away from the dust and noise of the grinding trucks.

The next morning we made breakfast and broke camp. Heading across the high plains we hit the road again and it was empty. On we went, this time enjoying the beauty of the scenery. The windows were rolled down but it started getting colder and colder as we gained altitude. The good old truck had a heater, which we had not used since Alaska, and it seemed it had forgotten how to work. I praise the Chevy often, as you have heard me say but it also took some "fixing" to keep it going, luckily it was easy to work on. Thank goodness I brought along my tools. We pulled over, looked it over and discovered it was just loaded with dust and dirt. We cleaned it and on it came, 'ah' warmth. The air was getting thinner and the temperature was dropping.

On the third day, at an elevation of about twelve thousand feet, the completely deserted road lay flat and straight. The gravel surface even looked good, so I stepped on the gas and brought it up above fifteen, to about twenty five miles an hour. Whoopee; we were moving along now. That was a mistake! At this speed we hit a deep pot hole, heard a loud crack and swerved off the road. Something serious had broken. Yep; serious. As I have mentioned this was a four wheel drive pickup truck. The front axle housing, on these three quarter ton trucks is cast steel with all the gears, slip fittings and axel shaft, inside this heavy 'banjo' casing. The axel housing is massive and strongly attached to the chassis to take the beating that comes with a 4x4. I guess we beat it too much; it was broken in half.

Please picture this scene; we are alone, twelve thousand feet in the high Andes, in the middle of nowhere, suffering from "soroche", the mountain sickness, with a broken truck and no one around to help. At least we thought no one was around. It was clear to me that we would be here for some time, so we set up a good camp site next to the truck. It was getting late in the afternoon and colder. I wanted to get started on the repair, or at least get a feel of what we were up against, so I got out the socket set and began taking off the front wheels. At these altitudes the air is so thin that you are out of breath in an instant, but even worse you get sick to your stomach with only a little exertion. I couldn't even turn the wrench a complete turn without throwing up. Not only that, but the blinding headaches stopped you cold. We were not getting out of here any time soon that was clear.

The next day we set about working on the truck in shifts. As one of us got sick another took over and gradually the bolts came off. Actually we were amazed that the bolts came off at all. On an old rusty truck, they usually get stuck. Having divided the work between three of us it left the one guy, not good at this, but very good at photography, free to wonder about and get some shots. Off in the distance a heard of Llama were grazing. What they were grazing on remained a mystery; there wasn't much to eat around here. We worked and he went off to get a closer look and hopefully some pictures. The day wore on and as I said, we got the axel off and were ready to go. Where and how we were going was anyone's guess, this was not I- 95.

It started to get dark and no sign of our photo mate. I don't know why you get so hungry at this altitude but you do, so we started a fire and began cooking supper. Suddenly our guy came stumbling into camp. He was out of breath and looked like he had seen a ghost. It turned out he had made it to the Llama herd and found two young Indian girls tending the flock. They were startled; they likely had never seen a white man before and they had never seen anyone that tall before; the Quechua Indians are short, the men are around five foot two or three, the women shorter, my friend was near six feet tall. Unlike our herding methods using horses or jeeps or dogs, they used a sling, "bolaros". The Biblical kind that David used to kill Goliath. It works pretty well, once you get the hang of it. They put a rock in the sling and throw it ahead of the lead llama to turn him in one direction or another. It saved running after them, no one wants to run at these elevations.

He told us what happened. As he approached the girls, they got frightened and ran. Calling to them in 'Spanglish' they stopped and the three of them sat down. As we had discovered many times before, young people are often too curious to be frightened for long. With little Spanish and no Quechua they had little to say. Our American representative decided to tell them about our moon landing by drawing a picture of the moon in the sand. He drew little stick creatures to represent the Astronauts and using his fingers showed them walking on 'La Luna'. The girls lived in a different world than ours, indeed in a different century and were not impressed with this strange white man. However they were fascinated by his camera and when he took it off to get some shots one of the girls grabbed it and started to run off. At twelve thousand feet they can run a lot faster and further then we can. He had no chance of catching them and gave up.

Back at our camp, the story of these events gave me some concern. I had heard that the Indians who inhabited these high mountains were not friendly to outsiders if they thought you were from the government or coming to tell them what to do. It was getting dark and I feared a surprise attack from the Indians, after the panicked story our camera man told of how they treated him. So I decided to do the John Wayne thing that I had seen in many of his movies and go directly into the tribal village and find the chief. We luckily had some great big down coats, brought from Boulder, and we dressed to look as large as we could. You know "might makes right". Two stayed with the truck, while our tallest member and I headed off toward the village, looking like over inflated balloons. There was one other John Wayne thing I remembered; bring a gift of some kind for the chief. What to bring; we had very little that would interest them. Ah-ha some soap; nice smelling soap. At the time I didn't know that these high altitude Indians never bathe in their entire lives, it's too cold and there are no vermin at this altitude.

It was easy to find the village. In the pitch dark of the mountain landscape it was the only fire light. The community consisted of a group of small stone huts in a circle with a stone fenced corral for the Llama. When we entered everyone had hidden in their houses, so I called out for the chief in my Spanish, not that they spoke much or any Spanish. Out came the tough looking Chief and his men, all looking tough, sticks in hand. I remind you again that we did not have any weapons with us on this trip, only our wits to get us out of trouble. The chief looked at me and me at him; I greeted him with my good old big smile and offered my hand. Hand shaking, as we do it, is not their custom, so he looked at me as if saying "what are you handing me". I then offered the soap and showed him, by putting it up to my noise, how sweet it smelled. Not realizing that they would never use it for bathing, it did smell nice. When he smelled it he called out the women who had been hiding inside, to smell it as well. They loved it! I have often brought great bottles of wine to parties stateside, but never got this kind of welcome for my gift. At this point one of the men held out our camera, that the girls had run away with, as his gift to me. Boy, that was easier than I expected. We all sat around the fire, which felt awfully good, and out came the coca. As I have mentioned before, coca is the drug of choice here in the Andes, the Indian men are high on it most of the time. You can't refuse it if offered; it would be a great insult to them. So chew some we did, it's awful, tastes like ripe silage. We didn't stay long but took the camera and headed back to camp.

Friends with the neighboring Indians turned out to be a pain in the neck. The next morning when we woke, our camp site was full of them, each looking for more gifts. Word had spread fast that gift givers were in the neighborhood and you better get over there before they run out of goodies. Having been raised in New York City, I was accustomed to beggars but these guys were leagues ahead of my city team. After a while we sent them on their way and got back to the business of fixing the truck.

THE GREAT AXEL REPAIR

Now What?!

Nice company

Just say NO to our Indian friends, we did, or more correctly kept saying 'no' till they finally left. Now to get the axel fixed. As I mentioned this front axle housing, banjo, was made of cast steel. For those of you who know about these things, you can't easily weld cast steel, to say nothing of being days away from any place with even electricity.

There it was, all one hundred fifty pounds of dead iron lying beside the truck and no means of getting it anywhere. There is no automobile club here, just us and the bitter cold and no oxygen. Suddenly, coming from the east, rising from the dust was a truck. Not just a truck but a big truck. This was the first vehicle to pass in three days. We flagged him down. These open bed, two ton trucks carry everything and everybody. It was coming from Cusco and headed to Arequipa, on the coast, just where I wanted to go. The Capital of Peru, Lima, is far from the coast and Arequipa is the big coastal city with a very active port that supplies the Capital.

The truck stopped and I explained what we needed. The driver said in Arequipa there were many shops that could fix the axle and he was heading that way and it would only take about two, maybe three days to get there. Great, only one problem, the back of the truck was already full of Indians and sheep. I was determined not to let this only ride go, so on we loaded the heavy axle and two of us. We left the other two guys to guard the truck till our return. Making room for us was not easy, all the good seats, there were no seats, only floor space, were taken by the Indians and the sheep. So we put the axle on the very rear end and placed ourselves between some sheep and it. Let me tell you, this is a bumpy road. If you have ever ridden in the back of a truck you know that the further back the more it bounces. As we bounced along, the axle started to bounce into some of the sheep and you should have seen them jump. Of course they jumped right on us sitting there on the floor; ouch, it hurt.

It became clear we could not survive this
way for several days and nights so we tied
the axle tight and worked our way up to the
'first class section' outside, over the cab, in
a box carrying the tarpaulins. Being up front
kept down the dust and the tarps made a
comfortable bed. We made good time no
breakdowns and no bandits; yes there were
lots of roadside bandits in those days. As we
approached Arequipa from above, I kept my
eye out for tall radio antenna. These were a
sign of a shortwave radio and with it contact
with the outside world. Often these radios
were at the homes of Catholic Priests, who
were missionaries on assignment from the
states. They also spoke English, even though
my Spanish was pretty good it was a lot
easier to explain what we needed in my
native language. The truck driver dropped
us off at the Priest's house and I paid the
driver what we had agreed and knocked on
the door. An ancient old Indian lady
answered the door and I asked for the
priest. She looked at me with my big red
beard and dirty face and dusty clothes and

must have thought I just had gotten down from a cross. The young Priest came out and I dived into English to tell him our plight.

What luck, he himself came from a farming family in the states and knew all about repairing trucks and tractors, so we compared notes. I told him that I sought him out because I saw the short wave radio tower on the house and needed to phone patch a call to Colorado to the General Motors headquarters in Denver to see about getting a new axle housing. Before I left Colorado, I made contact with the General Motors western headquarters, which was in Denver and got all the parts manuals for the Chevy Pickup. I got to meet the general manager for the entire region. He was so impressed with the planned trip that he gave me his private phone number. He told me that if I needed anything for the truck call his personal number and he would get it to me, no matter where I was. We made the phone patch call and believe it or not, we got through. My GM friend was amazed to hear from me and asked how we were doing and how he could help. I explained about the broken axle housing; he had never heard of one breaking before but said he could get it, only one problem, on that truck they used several different types and which one did I have. I didn't know, he said to look on the truck chassis to get the code. One problem the truck chassis was a week away round trip and no way was I doing that. I told him I'd get back to him and he wished us luck. Our Priest friend said he knew a machine shop nearby that did work on ship engines, so we drove over there. The place was gigantic, with lathes and presses that could do any job. The owner was a local guy who had gotten an engineering degree in the states and spoke English well, so I could shelve my Spanish for a while. He looked over the broken pieces and grinned. Looks like a clean break, no problem man. I don't think any sweeter words were ever spoken to me. He called his shop foreman and told him how to handle it and it was placed on a huge twenty foot long lath, on which they normally turned giant ship's engines crank shafts.

They carefully heated it first then welded it. On the lath they even heated it more so it could be straightened. In two hours it was done, good as new.

Strangers in a place like this can find great kindness from people newly met. After he heard the story of the trip and where we were headed, he insisted we come home with him for supper and a nights sleep in a real bed and would not accept any money for the work. The four of us, including the Priest spent a lovely evening with our engineer friend and after much wine and good food we hit the sack and slept the sleep of the dead.

At dawn our friend drove us and the axle to the beginning of the dirt road that led east to our truck. After a short while along came the very same truck we had used to get here and our now 'old' friend, the truck driver, greeted us like long lost buddies. Two days later we were back and immediately began putting the truck back together, all be it, slowly. The next morning, with the repair still not finished, a jeep came by heading west. In it was a missionary on his way to Lima. He was surprised to see U.S. American travelers, to say nothing of our condition and asked if he could help, nice guy. I said we had it under control now, when suddenly our two companions, who had stayed with the truck, jumped up and said they wanted to leave and ride with him to Lima. You find out who your friends are! I pleaded with them to stay and continue on the adventure. They looked at me and said this had been as much adventure as they needed for a lifetime, jumped in the jeep, wished us good luck and drove off. It was true, 'good luck' was what we needed. Off they went, never to be seen again, at least not around here.

The next morning we finished the repair and off we went. The truck was running well. With only two of us in the cab, before we had three, in the cab, with the fourth riding in the back, it was much more comfortable this way. At least there was some upside to losing them. Early the next day we were facing it, the highest navigable water in the world; Lake Titicaca, Twelve thousand feet in the Andes. What a sight. To us after so much time in the dry, dry high desert of the Alto Plano, seeing such a huge body of water seemed a mirage. The lake is twice the size of Rhode Island, 32,00 sq miles in size; an ancient inland sea, with floating islands. We were headed for a small village named Puno, where some Missionaries were stationed. Having been taught by Missionary Brothers in New York I wanted to see them.

We found them and I was very surprised to find a compound of men in their late twenties, like myself, living in great harmony with nature and very surprisingly with their families. They were all married, much against their vows of chastity. Here in the other end of the world, you take life differently than how you were raised back in the states. These guys were all here to introduce agriculture reform. Growing things and raising animals was their training and passion; along with producing crops they produced some kids of their own. All this by the way with the unofficial blessing of the head of their Order back home. They had officially left the Order but were kept on the payroll to keep the reforms going. What an interesting bunch of guys they were. Because of my background in New York, we had plenty to talk about. They were also fascinated about the travel adventures we'd had so far. I didn't know much about farming here but I did know plenty about their dedication to a cause and admired it greatly, as they admired my cause to get to the bottom of this great continent, South America. Here time stands still. A little thing like shearing sheep and the vicugna was lost or never known. These missionaries and some Peace Corps people introduced shearing of sheep, where before they killed the animals for their wool. This changed the entire economy of the high Alto Plano, now they had both the live animals and the warm wool.

HEADING NORTH TO MACHU PICCHU

Huayna Puchu guards Machu Picchu

The road to Cusco, the old Spanish Capital, is steep and as usual slow going. On we went, arriving in the small city in time for a festival. A religious march with lots of statues of saints. The marchers are predominately Quechua Indians with their mix of Catholic and ancient traditions. The statues of saints they were carrying didn't look anything like the ones I had seen as a child in our church. I guess if you want to convert people you need to make the 'Holy ones' look like the locals. All these saints were squat and very dark with long black hair, and looked local to me. Here in the high Andes, local people dress in very colorful outfits. All the women wear lots of fabric draped around themselves and the hats! The woman's hats are right out of the twenties. Black bolas and fedoras, they speak volumes about how time has stood still here. Pictures of the early archeologists, who came here, were wearing these styles and must have had an influence on them. Or they left their hats so they could make copies.

As night fell, things settled down and the place became pretty quiet. After only one day here I'm amazed at the architecture. Nowhere have I seen such incredible stone work. In all my growing up around the building business and the wonderful masonry of Manhattan Island, nothing compares to this. These buildings were built a long time ago without our modern machinery. The architects and the foreman of the work force must not have had construction unions to restrict the work load. The stones are gigantic and most impressive of all is that there is no mortar between the stones. Everyone who has seen any brick or stone structure has seen the mortar between the bricks to keep it glued together and level. These buildings and walls are held together by the sheer weight of the stones and the perfect cutting of each of them: they fit perfectly. Any union brick mason in the U.S. would be in awe of them.

After a few days here admiring the place and visiting lots of historic sites, it was time to take the next step. We planned to go to Machu Picchu and admire the great mountain fortress. It was just over fifty years since it was discovered and had not yet become the tourist attraction it is today. There is no road there. It is way up the Urubamba River and in those days the only way there was by steam engine railway. In South America almost everything seems to be UP hill. I guess some day with all this going up we will get to go down, but not yet. The mountains from Cusco go straight up and I mean straight up, the giant steam engine with its two cars, loaded with Indians and us, cannot go straight up but must make a series of switchbacks. Please picture this; you are sitting in an open window train car, looking nearly straight up over the car and the next set of tracks is there right above you. I know this is hard to imagine, but this is how the tracks are laid out, like a step ladder. At each switchback, the engineer would get off the engine. With a tin pot that had a very long spout on it he would put sand under the drive wheels of the engine for traction, for the next chug up to the top of the next switchback.

Up and up we went, even the locals were fascinated. After reaching the top, the train goes along a ridge for a while until the river appears along-side; and then the tracks and the river move along side by side towards Machu Picchu.

The Urubamba river valley is quite beautiful. It is steep, with sheer cliffs on either side. It is very defensible. Along the route there was not much to see except to be reminded that you were not in flat terrain Kansas. At the stop, at the base of Machu Picchu, there were many Indians, most with shovels and picks and working hard on what is now, I understand, a great tourist attraction. It was still a wilderness then. The ancient fortress is about two thousand feet above the river, and railroad. With our packs and sleeping bags on our backs we climbed to the top. Wow, what a sight. No wonder it took the Spaniards almost twenty years to find it and about seventeen years to conquer it; it's protectable. In fact it is said by military people that a modern army with modern hand guns could not take it today against defenders with only stones and spears. The Spanish did finally take it with use of a little subterfuge. Just as we had done with the

Indians who I thought were going to attack us, the Spanish made a friendship offering of some gifts and a 'Trojan Horse' and all got in. Then it was all over.

As I have said there was no one else besides us and some Indians cutting back the jungle from the stone ruins. There were lots of structures to see, all of them either still covered in bush or just cleared. As night fell, no one asked us to leave; no one cared that two bearded, tall, backpacking guys wanted to spend the night, except that they must be crazy. Everyone, except us, knew that there were spirits here and that they came out at night. Looking around for the best camp site we decided on a spot near what appeared to be the central plaza. From here we could see anything moving, anything with flesh or even without. Night came rapidly and the sounds from the valley and the hills and mountains around were different from the Alto Plano. There was clearly more life here. We were not anxious to meet any of it that night. It was cool and we slept well. Dawn broke and we had been spared any surprises during the night.

Across from our campsite were two strange stones: the big one, about the size of a Buick, sloped up to the west, like the front of a shoe with a donut hole near the top. The other end rose only slightly with a hole near its top. This stone was of great importance to the tribe. Here in the high Andes, winter is long lasting and nothing grows. In the southern latitudes, as you know, the seasons are the opposite from ours. Summer is winter and winter is summer. When on the winter solstice here, with the sun getting pretty low and lasting only a few hours per day, the people were getting worried. They thought that the sun might just go away forever; who knew! Who knew were the Priests. They had the best job in town. They had figured out the sun cycles and knew what was going to happen in a few days, the sun would gain strength again, and they just didn't want to tell anybody. On the shortest day of the year, people were in a panic, so they declared a holiday. With the magic hemp rope that they kept all year in a safe hidden place, at their place, they performed their great magic. With the nervous tax payers gathered all around they took out the rope and with the words only they knew, tied one end of the rope to the short end of the sacred rock and with the other end, as the last rays of sunshine passed through the west hole, they tied the other end to those rays and said the secret prayer.

The holiday lasted three days with fasting and praying to the Sun God. After three days low and behold the days started to get longer and the priests took the rest of the year off; with pay. Just for kicks, we took a nap on the great stone out of reverence or to show our respect for how clever they were.

The next morning, the workers returned on the train from their homes in Cusco and continued to clear the bush. We had been looking at the sheer jagged mountain peak that rises above the village. Huayna Puchu, a straight up climb about a thousand or more feet above us. We didn't need all our gear because we predicted a five or six hour trek. Like many things in life, it took longer than expected. We got up the top in reasonable time but we did not expect to find what we found. I guess no one had been up here for some time because they would certainly have seen the remains of the creature. I say Creature because it was not clear if they were human or something else. There wasn't much left but enough that said "this is not the best neighborhood to hang around in". Off the mountain we went. Unfortunately we screwed up and took a wrong turn and came to a sheer cliff, so we had to backtrack all the way back up. It was dark by the time we got back to camp in the Plaza. We had stored our stuff under some rocks so they were still intact. By this time the workers had gone home and there were no more trains till the next day, so one more night alone with the spirits was at hand.

Early the next morning we heard the train whistle blow and down the trail we went. Goodbye to this magic place and how happy we were, to be one of the last to sleep in it and feel the power of it. This is truly "THE MAGIC KINGDOM".

The Saints look like locals

MY DEPENDABLE CHEVY TRUCK

I have always depended on myself. I was raised by a single mom, my father died when I was five years old. Mom worked on Wall Street for fifty-five years, so as a consequence, my younger brother and I were taught to fend for ourselves. This is not to say mom was anything but kind and loving, but being latchkey kids we had no choice but to get our own lunch, see to our own needs and set our own standards. The Nuns and then the Jesuit and Marist Brothers naturally gave great guidance, as did my Mother's Yiddish father, Moses, who lived with us. We had the Jesuits in the day time and Moses at night. So it was not only the law of the New York City streets that guided us. The little I remember of my English Father, I was so young when he died, was that he told us because of our wonderful mix of ancestry, English, Irish and Jewish, "that we should speak British and think Yiddish", to get along in life, good advice. I guess in me this also lead to a desire to lead. We are all the package of the numerous things that go in in childhood, as am I.

The red Chevy truck on the other hand was made in Detroit with only the ancestry that I would give it. What a history it was receiving. Not many pickup truck's lives can match it. I bought the truck used in Boulder. It had been in an accident, so I got it cheap. The local high school had a body shop program for students and a friend of mine taught it. For only the cost of any new parts, you could get a first class body shop repair for almost nothing. You just could not be in a hurry for the finished product. After a number of months, the job was done and the 'new' shinny fire engine red, 4x4, three quarter ton, step side, long bed, 1962 Chevy pickup was done. At the time I didn't know that there was a crack in the front cast steel axle housing from the accident, as you have read in an earlier chapter.

Dependable is the word I use when thinking of the truck. It's funny, I have owned many sailboats and cars in my life and I always referred to them as 'she'. I never referred to the red truck as 'she'. It was always either 'the truck' this or that, or just the Chevy. I guess it has a special place in my mind, and nothing else since or before held that special place. Now please understand that it was not a new truck when I bought it and it got much more 'used' as we went along the journey. Let me tell you about some of the trouble it did cause.

Of all the things we brought along and all the things we forgot to bring along, nothing that we brought was as important as my mechanic's tools. I just remembered quite a story from Boulder. A week before we left on the trip, the local newspaper ran a story on our plans. A professor from the University called me and invited me to his house for a dinner party he wanted to have in my honor. I accepted and a few days later showed up at his place. There were about a dozen dinner guests there, all faculty members from CU. We had a wonderful meal and after dinner our host proceeded to show off a set of plans he had been working on for years on the same adventure I was about to undertake. I was amazed at the detail. Nothing like what I was bringing with me. He had the equivalent of another truck following him with backup supplies that could take care of General Sherman's Army as they marched south to Savannah. I guess he planned to stay hermetically sealed in the cab the whole way. I explained that unlike our gracious host I planned to be amongst the locals a great deal and we would deal with things as they came along. He was horrified; I was excited. The only thing I left his house with was a full stomach.

The first 'problem' with the truck occurred in Costa Rica. Costa Rica is a mountainous country. It is the only Central or South American Country, at the time, with a true democracy and no standing Army. As I said the country is very mountainous and to cross it there is a nine thousand foot pass to

cross. The 'road' is treacherous. A one lane
muddy rut with a few places to squeeze past
an oncoming truck. As we started up the
pass we got a flat tire. OK a flat tire, no big
deal. No big deal except there was no place
to pull over, just stop right there in the
middle of the one lane and fix it. The truck
had large split rim wheels on it and they
were tough to take off under good
conditions to say nothing of this. No sooner
did we start to fix it when a bus loaded with
uniformed police showed up behind us.
They were going over the mountain as well,
but not till we got out of the way and we
couldn't move in the mud. Many of them
got out of the bus to egg us on. I think it was
mostly friendly but I was not sure, except
to know they wanted us to hurry up. We did
the best we could and finally it was fixed
and off we all went. I let them pass when I
could. Like anywhere it is never comfortable
having the cops right behind you. The bus
driver was far surer of the road than I and he
sped off at a crazy speed. It was dangerous
in the daylight. It was suicide at night. The

next day we finally crossed and found a place to repair the tire. Bolted to the side of the truck were extra tires on rims but I wanted to have all the spares in good shape.

For those who have ever seen a big truck tire being fixed you will appreciate that it takes a lot of work to do it, but there are tricks to ease the job. I watched as the repair guys started to repair my tire with heavy hammers and pry bars. It takes forever to get the tire over the wheel rim if you don't know one of these tricks. I showed them how with the use of their ancient air compressor to blow it off by filling the tube with plenty of air till it popped. I was like a king to them after that. Drinks all around, Señor, 'para usted'.

There were a number of other repairs from time to time, most I fixed myself. There was one other repair that sticks out in my mind. Coming down some mountain pass in South America, we hit a big rock and broke one of the rear leaf springs. We limped along for the next few days with a seriously listing truck and finally made it to a town with some repair facilities. Now it turned out that Chevys are the most popular truck in this part of the world. So repairing them is very doable. Every mechanic is familiar with them and trusts them. I found a small blacksmith shop with some crude welding equipment and stopped. We jacked up the truck and the blacksmith and I crawled under it. He took out his old pipe wrenches to get off the spring. I told him to wait and I went and got my socket wrench set. He had never seen anything like it before and wanted to trade his beautiful daughter for the set. I said I was flattered but the sockets seemed more valuable on this trip. We welded the spring, I paid him and were off once again in the good old Chevy. I thought than that if I ever found a woman as reliable as this Chevy, I'd marry her.

THE HIGHEST CAPITAL

No flying over these!

La Paz is way up there, over twelve thousand feet above sea level and in the middle of nowhere. Bolivia is a land locked nation. It is the poorest in South America and that is saying something given that the neighbors are not exactly rich. It is surrounded by spectacular mountain peaks of over twenty thousand feet, so you still feel like you have not gotten there yet, even though you are not going any higher. The city sits on a level plateau, [well sort of level]. It is very busy with local people and Indians from the surrounding mountains. They are there to trade and look around at all the new wonders, such as electricity. Have I mentioned that these Quechua people have the largest lung capacity of any people on Earth? It is not surprising given how little oxygen there is in these parts. In the big outdoor market the Indians sell and trade all kinds of goods and plants. The most popular plant is coca. It is chewed constantly by the men. You see it dribbling from their lips everywhere you go. These men have a good deal, their only job, on these market days, is to carry the two hundred pound or so bundle to the market and open it , spread out the goods and chew coca the rest of the day. The women take over and conduct all the business. ----- Life is good!

By the time we got here the remaining two of us had been in some pretty good scrapes together. We had survived bullets, bandits and brushes with the law, but now it was time for my most trusted buddy to leave. I can't tell you how sorry I will be to see him fly out tomorrow. It isn't even the thought of being alone; it's how close we had become. He and I had been together since Alaska and the Yukon and I'd gotten used to seeing him every day. Wanting to do something special for our last day; we went to a little local bar, we had passed yesterday, to have a drink to our friendship and the great adventure we had shared. We got a seat by the open window so we could have a look at the people passing by. We raised a glass to our having survived all of what had passed in the last many months and to our friendship. Suddenly my friend stood up and yelled out the open window; 'STOP', in the loudest voice imaginable.

Let me back up to last night. We were camped, parked, in town in a quiet neighborhood, a few blocks from here. Sometime during the night, while we were sleeping in the back of the truck, someone broke into the truck cab, maybe we even left it unlocked, and stole his heavy wool lined handsome winter coat. It was one of those coats where the collar and the lapel have the furry white wool showing, very easy to spot. In any event, when he yelled 'STOP', there was his coat walking across the street from us. Out the open window he went and collared the guy, ripped off the jacket, as the thief flew down the road. It was sort of a last goodbye mini adventure. We sat back down and ordered some more beer and just grinned at each other; we had won once again.

The airport in La Paz is at an elevation, like the city, at almost twelve thousand feet. The air is so thin that it is built like an aircraft carrier, where the planes take off over a cliff, drop some, and then gain altitude. They sell a lot of rosary beads on these flights. My very good and trusted buddy was gone. Now, it's just me, the red truck and many thousands of miles still to go----alone.

Sometimes you meet the darndest people. The next day at the market I heard English being spoken. I found two long haired bearded, my age, American pilots. These were not your average American Airlines pilots with pressed white shirts and shoulder patches. Here were a couple of 'hippies' who happened to fly big airplanes and had one with them. As we know, La Paz is to the west of the highest peaks of the Andes. Some of these mountain tops rise well over twenty thousand feet. They are a sight to behold. The Capitol here has one problem; the small amount of grazing land around us, does not have sufficient grass for the cattle needed to feed the population. The large cattle herds are to the east, over the mountains, on the huge grazing lands of Trinidad, north of Cochabamba, and the surrounding countryside. Getting the beef here is a big problem. There are no roads through the mountains and if there were they would be impassable and lethal. We had lots of experience on 'death roads' high in other parts of the Andes to understand this all too well.

The 'Hippie' Pilots were part of the solution. They and some other 'brave'[i.e. foolish] guys flew old DC3 and DC6, World War Two, cargo planes over the 'hump', the mountains, to get the beef. Sounds doable till you realize they can't fly OVER the mountains. They are not capable of those altitudes. They fly between the mountain peaks. In this remote part of the world there are no radio beacons to guide them; they just fly by sighting up the valleys when they can see them and by stop watch when they can't. I'll explain in a minute.

The conversation was so interesting that the three of us went off to get some lunch. These boys seldom meet anyone else who is as adventurous as they were, so when they heard about my trip, they felt like we were contempories. At lunch they told me they were heading off to get a load of beef the next day and did I want to go for a ride. Did I want to go for a ride? You bet your life I did!

The next morning we met at the airport. We walked over to what looked like an old WW11 bomber. Inside there was nothing, don't even think about 'first class' or even 'coach', this was bare fuselage. The cockpit area was a basic as you can get. Some of the instruments were broken and others just ripped out. I once had a car like this, but I kept it on the ground. We were going to fly this thing. I guess they saw my concern and did the sensible thing, they pulled out some joints. Then told me to open my right hand with my fingers spread apart. Between each finger they put a joint, lit them all and said the best thing to do was puff on all of them. The higher I got now, the better I would feel when the plane got high. Soon after, all of us were high; in the air.

That day the sky was clear so the trip, which took several hours, was reasonably smooth. I was sitting in the third seat in the cockpit which, in the old days, was for the navigator. The mountain peaks rose majestically and menacing around us, as we flew down a valley. Looking out of the little side window near my seat I could see how rugged this area is. Every now and then you could see the wreckage of airplanes scattered across a mountain side. This was not very reassuring, but on we went. Late in the afternoon we landed at a dirt landing strip, in the middle of what looked like a giant ranch. The country side is very different from the western side of the Andes. We were surrounded by lush pastures and the greenest grass you have ever seen. The cows were happy here, till the butcher showed up. My pilot friends knew everyone and we were driven off in

an old jeep to the ranch house. Talk about a
Hacienda. This place would have been
Ponce de Leon's dream spot. In the court
yard was my favorite breed of horse, which
I now have several myself, Paso Fino. These
four gated beauties are said to be one of
the reasons the Spanish conquered South
America. In their smooth Paso gait they do
not arch their backs and allowed a Spanish
soldier to stay in the saddle and fight for
hours. This is where we were going to
spend the night. Dangerous as the flight is
in daylight, it's completely lethal at night.
We ate and drank to all hours before falling
asleep in one of the grand bedrooms. In the
morning I was pleasantly surprised to find
that our 'Captain' and his co-pilot were
perfectly sober. After breakfast we headed
to the airstrip. The plane was fully loaded
with tons of freshly killed beef hanging on
hooks and stacked on the floor. It smelled
like the butcher shop it was. Off we went
high above the pampas up into the
mountains. I mentioned that our trip here
had clear weather, now it started to sock in.

As the mountains got nearer we could see almost nothing, then suddenly we could see nothing at all. Our co-pilot calmly took out a stop watch and yelled out to the Captain to turn left three degrees. Holy mackerel, they were flying by stop watch, blind, in-between twenty thousand foot mountains. I took comfort in their calm attitude with each other. I assumed they did not want to die any more than I did, so I closed my eyes and hoped for the best. We were going along, with every now and then a break in the clouds. When the clouds opened all you could see was that those solid rock mountains were right next to us. Below in the valleys you could also see the wreckage of airplanes that had not made it. At one point, in blind cloud cover, they started to argue over how many degrees to turn. I thought this is it, we're goners. Nothing happened and after a few more terrifying hours we landed safely back in La Paz. No more flying for me, I'm going back to driving.

A NEW RIDER

9,000 miles at 15 mph

Life and Death

I was driving in La Paz, when I saw a big
blonde headed guy hitch hiking. I stopped
to pick him up. He was on holiday from
Austria and hoped to get to Argentina. His
English was so-so, but we could understand
each other well enough to strike a deal. At
this point I was running out of money, I
used travelers checks from the states, but
there weren't many left. He had money he
planned to use for whatever transportation
he could find, and I had the best transport
of all; the red Chevy truck. Again as
happened in Alaska with the two hitch
hikers there, luck came my way in the nick
of time. He had checked into a small hotel,
so we gathered his things and loaded them
into the truck. He had traveler's checks as
well and whatever the agreed amount of
the deal was, I don't remember now how
much, he signed that amount over to me.
The next morning we were off, heading
south once again.

From here the going was mostly downhill.
There were some long stretches of flat
ground, but most often it was down narrow

steep, dangerous dirt and gravel tracks. On one of the flat places I asked my new companion if he could drive. He said yes. I pulled over and he took the wheel. In two minutes he lost control and over the edge we went. Luckily it was not a big drop and the good old truck did not turn over. He then admitted that he had only driven once before and that too ended in disaster. I drove from then on. The snow capped peaks create a lot of water running down the mountain sides. At one point, around a bend, was a local car wash. No, not the drive in kind with the automatic hook that pulls you through with soap than rinse cycles. There was only one cycle here. It was, a waterfall dumping directly onto the side of the narrow road. We pulled into it and gave the truck a good bath. In the high Andes these narrow roads are two way. They cling to the sides of the cliff with no room to pass another vehicle, except here and there where there's a pull over. The drops on the outside are often hundreds of feet straight down. Not many live through these accidents here and I was determined not to be the next statistic. The road switches back and forth so that you can see some distance ahead. The unwritten rule here is that a vehicle going downhill has the right of way. The thinking is that going down your brakes might fail or heat up so much that you can't stop. So the one coming up looks for a place to get out of the way.   If he or you can't find one, then it's a tricky game of squeeze and pray, neither one wanting to be the guy on the outside, cliff side.

We were going along at about fifteen miles an hour, in second gear, with the familiar whine of the transmission, when we came around a curve and there upside down was a truck at the bottom of a ravine. There were bodies lying around the truck and miraculously some dazed people standing there as well. We stopped as did another truck coming up the other side. To us this was horrifying; to the local truckers it was common. We all climbed down to see what help could be given. Several people seemed

OK, but a few were apparently dead. As we administered some drinking water to those who needed it, we helped remove the others from the crushed cab. Over the next few hours others arrived and aided in pulling the bodies up the cliff. It was getting late, when no more could be done, we got back in our truck and wished those who remained; "Buen a suerte", good luck.

When you are raised in a country like ours in the U.S., death is confined to television shows and the movies. Here it is almost an everyday occurrence. Driving off we were shaken. When you are on the scene you are thinking of the help you are giving and don't think of the whole disaster. Later sitting calmly, it hits you. You also realize that but for the grace of God; that could have been you. It wasn't, so on we went.

On these high mountain roads there are very few places to stop and refuel and get a drink. Before dark we lucked out and found a wide place in the road that had a little village, so we stopped and took a break.

There were other trucks there and we talked about the accident. Again we were amazed with the matter of fact way they looked at things like death and near death. I guess if you live in this dangerous part of the world, you better get used to it.

As we got closer to the Argentine border, the mountains died away and the driving was not as exciting as it had been. Here the biggest worry was hitting someone on the road side. The place was loaded with horses, donkeys, bikes, scooters, walkers and the usual trucks. There must be good rain fall here because the farms seem rich in produce. The green fields are full of stooped workers gathering the harvest. The donkey carts are all about and the standing still ones have very content donkeys, sound asleep, waiting to be annoyed by their drivers whacking them, so they will unwillingly move. Unlike the donkeys, the people seem to be very willing workers. Maybe the donkeys really run the place and have trained the humans to do the hard work; looks that way. We took our time and enjoyed this rich environment after the white knuckle driving of the past many days. My Austrian passenger's English was getting better, or my ear for his English was improving. In any event we could now have longer talks. It is more enjoyable to share the experiences with someone else, then to be alone, talking to yourself.

As usual, the border showed up suddenly and as usual it was armed with Guardia National troops and their machine guns and other hardware, of which they were very proud. As with the other experiences with the Army, I'm never sure how much ammo they have and what kind of training they have received. They are masters at wearing the uniforms, especially the officers. The outfits are clean and well pressed and adorned with different badges of rank and achievement. After the shooting border war back in Honduras, I'm also not sure if they can shoot straight. There seem to be plenty of birds here, a sure sign they have not had a border war for some time. This border is on a small river, or creek, as we would call it, so there is no question of which side of the border you are on. Still on the Bolivian side, I had a great conversation, in Spanish, with a local 'ganja' seller. I had no need for any 'smoke' but he was telling me that over there, in Argentina, a mere hundred feet away, his product was very expensive and illegal, and so I should stock up now. Back in Central America and the jungles of this continent, weed is sold in cigar size; they are classed as one hand or two hand heft. We saw some as big as a large bratwurst. They are big enough that it takes two hands to hold them or small enough that one hand will do. I guess if you are working, the one hand one is needed so you can use the other hand for the job. I declined, but was very pleased with my Spanish speaking abilities.

Well it was time to cross into the last country on the route, though still with thousands of miles to go.

ARGENTINA, A DIFFERENT SOUTH AMERICA

Stamp, stamp, stamp and we were out of Bolivia. We crossed the little 'international' bridge that connected, or separated, the two counties. The Argentine border post was a contrast to the ramshackle posts of most of the other countries. It looked modern and organized and most of all, very Military. We rolled up in the rough Chevy, dirty and dusty and looking like a couple of vagabonds. Now looking like 'hippie' vagabonds never bothered any of the border guards before, however now it was not a recommended look. Just because we both had great, uncut, red beards, dirty shirts and pants, and only I spoke Spanish or English, the guards proudly spoke some English. Plus my guy had a passport from Austria, which they had not seen before. All the above did not make them excited about letting us enter their country.

Not only our looks, but my Spanish, of which
I had become so proud, did not serve
me well. Standing at attention in front of the
well-armed guards, with machine guns
pointed at us, they did not seem to
understand me. Their Spanish was very
different than the Spanish I had been
speaking for many months. I knew I was not
speaking any differently from before. In fact
I looked across the border, to the Bolivia
side and there was the Bolivian with whom I
had just had a fluent Spanish conversation.
What's up with this Argentine Spanish?
Enough was understood by both sides that I
finally persuaded them that my Austrian
friend was not an escaped Nazi and we were
not trouble makers from up north. A ranking
officer came over, heard my defense of our
adventure and where I had started my trip,
verified by all the stamps on my passport,
and ordered his soldiers to let us enter.
Once again I felt like we had just escaped
from the Gestapo.

Northern Argentina was a step back in time.
The very name Argentina means 'silver' as

discovered by early Spanish explorers. Not a time capsule like the remote sixteenth century Andes, but a step back to the early nineteen hundreds of rural America. Horses were everywhere along the road. We were heading eastward in the direction of Buenos Aires, on the Atlantic coast, and still a long way off. The road itself was a much better gravel road then any we had been on in the other countries. It was a true two lane affair, being gravel it naturally did not have yellow lines so who had right of way was always a 'steering wheel debate'. Once again the big rock guard that had served so well on the Alcan Highway to and from Alaska, caught a lot of stones, thrown up by passing trucks, that otherwise would have come right through the radiator or the windshield and gotten us. We motored on.

I mentioned that we were struck by the simple technology of the rural farming we saw. The fields were full of workers and their historic equipment. Now you know that I am from New York City, born and raised. This does not, by itself, give one a great knowledge of farming. In fact in my upbringing I thought that all food came from the A&P supermarket, it was already wrapped and had a price tag on it. I thought it came that way from nature. Well OK, I am exaggerating a bit.

Actually my first College enrollment was in Animal Husbandry, a preveterinary medicine program, at one of New York State's Universities. I had an uncle who had a dairy farm and in summers I spent time there and loved it. Getting my hands dirty and dealing with cattle was a natural for me. At school we had barn duty before class. Crossing the campus at four in the morning in freezing cold weather to milk cows and feed chickens, etc. was a chore gladly done. In fact I liked this work more than I did class work.

I came to know, in my time there, that doing this for the rest of my life was probably not for me. It did leave me with a great love for the life of the farmer and an understanding of farming practices. Here though, were farming practices that way predated even my school experiences.

In the fields, not only were there lots of people working but pulling harvesters and other equipment were teams of oxen and mules. The movie memory of the twenty mule team pulling the Borax Soap powder wagon comes to mind. This image of the 'old west' was a living and breathing thing right in front of us. They were not making a movie; they were living their lives in real time. Why things had remained stuck in the turn of the twentieth century, I don't know. Argentina is a progressive place, loaded with people from all over the world, especially Germany and Italy, two countries that entered the early part of the twentieth century with a 'bang'; you could say. There they were, hard at it, in the bright South American sun light.

Driving along with other trucks on the road had become familiar since Alaska. Driving with horses on the road was common here.

Driving along with people walking beside the road was very common. Driving along with teams of oxen and mules pulling rows of wooden wheeled wagons loaded with produce was something I had never seen before. By the way, they do not move very fast. Passing them is almost impossible because they are so long and the dust they create prevents you from seeing far enough ahead. The one thing you can say is, they are friendly folks. Often sitting on the last wagon is a rider. I'm not sure if he was a hitch hiker or part of the wagon train, but he would always be facing back, looking right into our windshield. This was sort of a no words meeting. Often we and he would use friendly hand gestures to communicate. Mostly they would give us the universal hand sign for cigarettes, you know, two fingers in a 'V' put up to your lips. We didn't smoke, so 'NO' is another one of those easy, universal head shakes. Even my Austrian buddy felt like he was speaking Spanish; well sort of!

The destination of the wagon trains was the nearest grain silo or farmstead. In any event suddenly they would veer off and the road would open again. Like a sled dog team, only the lead dog has a decent view, as was our case. Without one of them right in front of us the view improved dramatically. It was beautiful country all around. South East we went.

The National Geographic map of this, more modern country, is quite good. The little villages along the way are accurately noted. From time to time we would stop in one or another for a break and to get the local flavor. They always had fresh fruit and squeezed juice drinks for sale. They, like many of their neighbors in the countries north of here, sell stuff. They are a very entrepreneurial people. Their enthusiasm when you come to one of their food and drink carts is contagious. I could never keep a smile off my face, when faced with the smiles on theirs.

Cordoba is getting closer. This will be the first 'big' city in a long time. We are looking forward to some 'real' restaurants and city life. Cordoba had a population of around three quarters of a million people. It is the second largest city in Argentina. Located near the foot hills of the 'Sierras Chinas' mountains, it is hot and humid, semi tropical. It is a beautiful city but too big for my Austrian friend. He was petrified of all the traffic and the hub bub of the place, me I loved it. We did not stay very long. We headed for the city of Rosario, in the north central part of Argentina. The driving got easier, with a well maintained, paved surface. For the first time, we hit third and even fourth gear. We were flying now.

JAIL TIME IN ARGINTINA

Heading east, south east, and the country side continues to be verdant farming country. The green landscape is very pleasing to the eye. Pleasing as well are the vast number of horses and Caballeros, riding with great skill amongst the cattle and farm steads. I have always loved horses. As a child, growing up in New York City, we never had any dogs or cats in our apartment. The only living thing in the apartment, besides ourselves, were guppies in a fish bowl. I did however have a horse, no, not in the apartment but in a riding stable on the upper west side. In fact it was the oldest riding stable in America. Well over one hundred years old in the same location. Now, like most people in New York, he lived in a six story building. In fact my horse, along with others, was on the sixth floor. We would put him, he was a gelding pinto, in the elevator and take him down to the first floor, saddle him up and ride over to Central Park. So from horses I know, and love them.

The Caballeros are fine horsemen. They not only ride well, they look the part as well. Their outfits are all cowboy, at least cowboy as viewed here. They were more of a Clint Eastwood look then a John Wayne look. They had more scarves around their necks and waists then a belly dancer has.

It was getting dark and we found a small puebla, [village] to stop at. It turned out to be Saturday night and the village was hopping. There were a few roadside bars near the center, so we sat down at one and ordered a beer. The locals were not used to having strangers with them and were very curious. I told the group around us at the bar, about where we were from and where we were headed. They clearly had never been to Alaska or even the U.S., in fact almost none had ever been to the next big town. So there was the familiar look of curiosity but no real understanding, much like the high mountain Indians on the 'moon landing day'. They were very proud of their traditions however. Suddenly we heard the thunder of a horse heard coming down the road. We looked around and there was the eighteenth century coming toward us, at a gallop. Try to picture this, maybe twenty horsemen riding erect in the saddle, wearing beautiful Spanish cowboy outfits, dressed to the nines, caring long lances. Was it King Arthur? No; this is the traditional Saturday night entry of these working ranch hands; we were told they do it every weekend. What a sight. We never had this on any Saturday night in Manhattan. They dismounted and drank with us and the other folks at the bar. A good time was had by all. We stayed the night and set off in the morning, not till very late morning when our heads were clear; thank you.

As we got further and further into the country, the farming and ranching equipment got more and more modern. No longer were there mule teams pulling wagon trains, but now farm tractors doing the job. There were fewer and fewer horses and Caballeros on the roads. It was as if we were time traveling from the eighteen hundreds, to the present, in only a few days. What a fascinating experience this was. In almost the blink of an eye, one hundred years had passed by.

Heading east, we came to a cute little city, or you might say a big town, named Rosario.

This was much more to the liking of both of us and we decided we would really explore the place. Little did I know what I would be exploring very soon? It was time to fill up the many gas tanks on the truck, so we found a gas station. Now, unlike the remote 'gas stations' in the mountains and deserts, this was a 'state side' look alike. I think we took about thirty or forty gallons and it was cheap. Gas had gotten as low as nine cents a gallon in places and here it was something like twenty cents a gallon. We filled up. This being a Sunday there were few people around, I guess most were in church. It happened that the owner was there and I did the usual math to convert my U.S. money orders to Argentine pesos. I was pretty fast and accurate with the math and prided myself on it. I handed the gas station owner the correct number of traveler's checks. Remember we are not far, one hundred miles or so from Buenos Aires, a huge very modern city, the owner looked at the traveler's checks, said NO Señor, and demanded 'local' money. I didn't have enough to pay for the gas and a heated argument ensued. I yelled that even the most remote Indians in the Alto Plano would accept these traveler's checks. Are these Indians smarter then you!? He didn't like that; by the way, my Spanish was good enough to have this hot argument. Suddenly two police cars roared onto the scene, called by the gas station assistant, and three of us were wrestling on the ground. Me, a cop and the gas station owner. In the melee, the keys for the truck fell out of my pocket and as they handcuffed me and dragged me away, they told my Austrian friend to follow in the truck. I tried to tell the cops that the keys were on the ground but couldn't remember the Spanish word for 'keys'. Luckily my guy saw them and followed.

I cannot recommend jail under any circumstances and certainly not in South America. Just like you see in the westerns, there were iron barred cells along a wall. I guess they felt sorry for me and gave me a separate one. Perhaps they thought I was a trouble maker and didn't want me making trouble with the other prisoners. Slam, click, click and I was locked up tight. What about 'Miranda rights' or one call, or I want a lawyer; good luck on 'your rights', you don't have any! This jail was a small place, so all of us were in sight of each other. I had in my pocket the journal I was keeping and started writing in it. I called out to the 'desk sergeant', who was right across the room from me and asked the name of 'El Jefe', the chief. The officer was surprised and asked why. I told him I was a newspaper reporter from the States, indeed from, Nueva York, the New York

Times newspaper doing a story on Rosario
and the world would soon see how awful
this city was to visitors and I asked him
once again for his name for the article.
"Que es esso" and he picked up the phone
and called the chief. About an hour later
the 'Chief', in all his finery showed up. He
had a little talk with the guard and came
over to me and asked about the newspaper
story. He had been to New York he said and
knew 'my' fine newspaper and insisted all
this had been some big mistake. He gave
me the spelling of his name and his rank
and said he looked forward to reading my
story. As he was letting me out of the cell,
along came the gas station owner to press
charges and the Chief grabbed him and
threw him in the cell I had just moments
before occupied. Apologies were all around
and we were given a royal police escort out
of town. I'm sure they let the gas guy out
once we were gone. Ah, Life was good
again! Once again luck and wit had saved
my skin.

Sometimes the best weapon is inside
yourself, not hanging in a holster.

BUENOS ARIES-A REAL LIVE CITY

As we have seen Argentina was far more modern then most of the rest of South America, at least it was then. Buenos Aires had a population of three and one half million people then. By comparison New York City had a population of around eight million. Three and one half million is still a big city! Driving into the city is a delight. The roads are paved properly and there are even yellow lines for the different lanes. A First Class place. It's hard to imagine we are on the same continent with the wild primitive places that lay to the north. I didn't mention that I was suffering from an infection between two of my fingers where I had been cut by a knife back in Bolivia. It was a relatively minor thing at first but with the poor diet of 'mountain soup', consisting mostly of things the Indians found lying around, my fingers had gotten infected. I needed some protein. Argentina and Buenos Aires in particular, is noted for their steak. There is lots of beef around. Driving here we had seen lots of it on the hoof. Now I wanted to see some on the dinner plate.

My Austrian friend was ending his journey here and he planned to ship out in a few days. At this time the U.S. dollar was strong. I forget the exact exchange rate, or how many of theirs you got for how many of ours, but I know, you got a lot of theirs for only a few of ours, especially in the black market. Sorry, but I loved the black market. To splurge we decided to rent a couple of hotel rooms for a few days. The rate for two rooms, was about one dollar per day, cash only, no receipt. It looked like some of the girls in the neighborhood like this hotel as well. Though they never seemed to stay for very long. Perhaps they didn't like the other guests or something. We checked in and on the advice of the hotel clerk found a local beef restaurant. The place was fantastic. It was a local hang out, but upscale with linen table cloths and linen napkins. I had not used anything but my sleeve while eating for some time, so this was a treat. We ordered a craft of good Argentine red vino and polished it off in no time. I guess it was a Malbec but I couldn't have cared less what grape it came from. The menu was extensive. Red meat of all descriptions was on the menu. Seated behind us were three local men with plates loaded with blood red meat filling their plates. I ordered one like that, pointing to them. We stuffed ourselves and went back to the hotel and fell into a deep sleep.

The truck was parked at one of the grand plazas nearby. As I had done many times before in other countries, I hired a local guy to guard it. Before I choose this particular guy, I asked around as to who was the toughest and most reliable of the 'guards' who had offered to watch it. There was never a shortage of 'watchers' available for hire, but you always wanted the toughest one because he controlled the turf. The next day my Austrian truck mate boarded a freighter bound for Europe and home. We parted good friends and happy to have shared so many rich experiences together. Now alone again, with still about three thousand miles to go, I reassured myself that making it to the bottom 'had' to be done. God I wanted to end it right now and go home.   But I did not!

The camper shell, or more accurately the big metal box in the bed of the truck, had a large map of North and South America drawn on it. I had progressively extended the red line down the countries as we came south. It now was pretty impressive running all the way from the Arctic Circle to here in BA. One day I was sitting on the tailgate and a newspaper reporter came by. He had seen the truck and the map the day before and wanted to interview me about the trip. Like every meeting he offered to buy lunch at a local bistro and I said 'si, por supuesto', { yes, of course]' and off we went. Over the usual bottle of good wine, I think it was afternoon by then, well maybe not, we talked. I gave him all the GORY details along with many of the GLORY details and he said if his editor agreed it would appear in the

Sunday feature section of the paper.
Sunday came and I was featured alright.
The front page had a picture of me and the
red truck, with a caption, followed by a
bunch more pictures and long story in the
front of the features section. Instantly I
became a star. People started coming to the
Plaza to see the truck, the map and even
me. Best of all some pretty girls came by as
well.

Perhaps you know that BA has a lot of first
and second generation Germans and Italians
living there. At this time beards were
very unusual. Men were clean shaven
so my very large red beard stuck out, to say
the least; fortunately once again, girls
seemed to like it. I didn't mind at all. Two
sisters came back a few times and we had
wonderful conversations. They were so
interested in hearing about the U.S. and the
Beatles and the other 'hippies' and free love
and you know what teenage girls think
about. They invited me to their parents'
home for dinner. I accepted. The next
evening they showed up and we took the

subway to their house. At the door their very Germanic father let us in. Mom was in the kitchen preparing the meal, but came out to get introduced. I speak no German but my Spanish was good and probably sounded as heavily accented as did theirs. Mine with an English accent, theirs with a German one. We had not spoken but a few words when in booming voice the father let me know they had come here to Argentina in "sirty nine" [39], and that Hitler was a SOB. In the coming days I met other German people and every one of them made it clear they came here in "sirty nine". I guess in thirty nine, all of Germany must have emptied out before the war, and come here. I expect the '39' passport stamp was kept in use, for certain people, long after thirty nine had passed.

Besides pretty girls, others came by to offer support for my remainder of the journey. One group was the Automobile club of Argentina. I had noticed their many storied high rise building downtown and was impressed with its design. Officials of the

club came by to ask if they could host a
reception in my honor at their headquarters
the next evening. Many of their members
had seen the newspaper story and wanted
to meet me. I explained that I did not have
very proper clothing for a formal affair and
they insisted I come as the explorer they
envisioned me as. The next night was
fantastic. The two story entry lobby, where
the party took place, was awash in good
wine and fine food. The 'hoy poly' of BA
were there, including many of the "thirty-
niners" I mentioned before. At an
appropriate moment the President of the
Club rang a bell and all fell silent. He
mounted a podium and after a few words
introduced me. A round of applause, how
nice. I then proceeded to tell them they had
a problem. As I mentioned the main huge
entry room where we were, had a marble
map running around the vast space
depicting the, not yet built "Pan American
Highway". It was wrong! I could not stop
myself from pointing a huge error. Even
though it was not yet built, it was supposed

to follow the dirt track I had taken all these many thousands of miles. There was NO road where they showed it. They were polite and after hearing some of my stories they gave me a big hand and a good time was had by all. I'm sure if I go there today it will still show the same wrong alignment. It cost a fortunate to change a two story marble wall, right or wrong and the likelihood of any of their members driving it were remote. Once again it was time to get on the road.

THE ARGENTINE ALPS

Our Summer; Their Winter

Heading out of Buenos Aires is as modern as the US. They are a very organized people and their roads show it. Over the many years I have lived in the Caribbean, where the roads are awful, I believe that indeed roads reflect the culture of the place. Worldwide it is often a condition of 'some of the nicest people you will ever meet, with the worst roads you could ever imagine'. Argentina has the luxury of fine people and fine roads, how unusual. At the southern end of the city, I stopped to gas up the truck. As I was standing there a car full of well-dressed men approached me. After the gas station incident in Rosario I was on guard, are they police or relatives of the jailed gas station owner still mad at me, I wasn't sure. The driver got out; he was a man in his mid-twenties wearing a suit and tie. He handed me his business card and introduced himself as a member of the Automobile Club at which I had given the talk the other day. He said how impressed he and the others were with my adventure and wished to invite me on a hike he and his other friends were going on the next day to the 'Delta region'. His card showed that he was the President of the Argentine Hiking Association. He explained that it was a large group of active people who monthly hiked to interesting places and the Delta was indeed very interesting. I hadn't been there and said I would be happy to go, he said to meet them at the main train station tomorrow, at precisely seven in the morning and be prepared for a good long hike.

Feeling like I was representing the U.S. in the Olympics and not wanting to let my new reputation as an 'international adventurer' slip, I went to sleep early and drank lots of fruit juice that night, to be in my prime for the arduous upcoming hike. I did not want to let my country down. I was also a member of the Colorado Mountain Club and I would show them how we hiked in the Rockies.

The next morning I arrived early at the Station, no one was there yet. I waited, seven passed, no one, eight o'clock, no one, was I in the wrong place, was it a joke on me, I didn't know. Finally at close to nine dozens of "hikers" showed up. They were only fashionably late. Each of them was dressed to the nines with matching berets and sport jackets with an emblem emblazoned on the front and ascots neatly tucked. Needless to say I was the least well dressed. Each one also handed me their official 'hiking club' embossed business card. We boarded the train and two hours later were hiking down a well-marked trail for about ten minutes to what look like a picnic area already set up with tables and benches. Out came the wine and the sandwiches and the 'hiking' was over, almost before it began and it was time to eat and drink. So much for the rugged 'hiking club of Argentina'. The next day I headed south for some real adventure.

A few hundred miles south of BA is the magnificent Switzerland of Argentina— Bariloche in Rio Negro. The town is otherworldly, compared to everything else in South America. The buildings are right out of Disney, The stone civic center is Vail Colorado, the Stone churches could be anywhere in Bavaria. I wish my Austrian friend could have seen this. The official name of the city is 'San Carlos de Bariloche' named after one of the first nineteenth century settlers. The guy's name was Carlos from Bariloche. Bariloche means "people of the other side of the mountain", makes sense to me. It is very German. The German people came here in the 1890's, they liked it and stayed. In fact it was said that Hitler and Eva came here after the war and were part of the community till someone noticed his mustache and turned him in. Probably not true. However two U.S. desperados did live here for several years, between 1901 till 1905, before they too were run off; they were Butch Cassidy and the Sundance Kid. IT'S TRUE, I saw the movie; I know. The place is beautiful. The Cordillera de los Andes rise above the Steppe in a powerful mantle of Mountains kissing the sky as they swirl their snow caps towards the heavens.

It's another Magic Kingdom.

About sixty years before I arrived, Swiss pilgrims came here and started skiing. The snow is great for many months of the year and the Swiss cheese is good all year round. I got a real kick out of some people wearing 'lederhosen', but no one 'yodeled' thank goodness. I'm teasing about the place, I really did enjoy myself here. It was a great escape from all that had passed. The biggest problem was it made me very home sick for Boulder.

Dead south now to the border. Argentina is disconnected from its part of Tierra del Fuego because of the way Chile cuts across the Straits of Magellan. It's weird. In any event I was soon to cross into Chile. The road down the coast is uneventful. It's kind of boring compared to things like the 'death roads' of the Andes. I kept on till I reached the now familiar sight of the flags, the guns and the guards. Stamp, stamp. Stamp and cross. A few hundred feet more and stamp.

Stamp. Stamp. Stamp. Cross. There is not much of Chile to see. This is the 'nothing' tip of main land Chile. It's the 'side of the side road' as Arlo Guthrie said, but this is the way south.

After what seemed like no time at all I had 'crossed' this piece of Chile. It's hard to think of anything to say about the place. It was gone in an eye blink. It's like some of the states you pass through when crossing the US. I always wanted to see more of West Virginia when heading across on US 70. There is only the kiss of it in Wheeling and like here some yearning to look around but you keep going. Arriving at the ferry dock you have company for the crossing of the Straits of Magellan. Most of the things people living on Tierra del Fuego require are shipped over for both the Chilean and Argentine section of the island. The crossing itself is uneventful, except to realize where you are and then, how few have done it. The water is pretty flat, after all there is land on all sides and the wild Atlantic and Southern Pacific are held at bay by the land mass of the tip of South America and the island of Tierra del Fuego and the numerous other smaller islands.

On and off are easy, with a little more of Chile to go before the border the re-crossing happened in no time. All the usual papers, and getting the required stamps. Stamp, Stamp, Stamp; Cross. After all these border crossings I feel I could apply to be a Border Agent somewhere, I know just what is required and how to keep from smiling.

Well, well, well, Argentina again. I've crossed the Argentine border so many times I feel like they should know me by now; they don't, so get out all the papers once again. Here they are friendlier than at other crossings, perhaps because they feel anyone who has made it this far deserves some kindness and a grin.

THE BOTTOM AT LAST

Tierra Del Fuego—THE LAND of FIRE. It has been so long that I didn't know what to think. Ushuaia lay a little way ahead but this was it, the last piece of road, the last piece of land, the bottom; the END.

The land of fire! I wondered why they named it so, till I read about it. Then I saw it. Driving along the near coast dirt, sandy, gravely route, I saw in the distance a huge red glow. Fire, a lot of fire. On the horizon natural gas was burning. The land has great volumes of gas under it and it catches fire frequently with a glow so bright that there is no other name anyone would give to this place other than "Land of FIRE"! Perhaps thousands of years ago the native people living in the cold parts of Chile and Argentina used this like their 'Miami Beach' in winter. "Let's go warm up at the burning fire land," soon changed to Tierra del Fuego. It's possible; remember humans don't change that much from millennium to millennium.

The little fishing village of Ushuaia, is tucked, no huddled, in a valley that empties into the roaring southern sea. No one in the world lives further south. Forget the scientist who occasionally stay for periods on the ice of Antarctica. This is the southernmost place in the world that humans live! I was happy to have made it. There were many times that I thought that I would not get here. There were many times, over this tough journey, that I thought I didn't care if I did make it. Now I am pleased with myself and pleased with the companionship and friendship of my former traveling mates. I am standing here, ALONE, facing the Sea and Antarctica for all of you guys as well. Thank you for your contributions. Yes, I traveled the last several thousand miles alone, but it was all of us who "COUNQUERED THE BEAST'!

In those days the town, or village of Ushuaia, was quite small. When I got there a half century ago it was inhabited by many Yugoslavians who were excellent fisherman. In these rough seas you first had to be a

216

great sailor and boatman before you got a chance to fish. The collision of the Southern Atlantic and the Southern Pacific oceans create a violent waterway. The reason for creating the Panama Canal, a hundred years ago, was to avoid this dangerous place. There is a report of one very large sailing vessel beating against these waters for over two months and finally giving up and turning around and sailing back the other way around the world to complete its voyage. No sea Captain does this without good reason. It is said to be the world's wildest water.

On my first day there, I looked around and found it to be a very organized community. The Argentine Government maintains a military base here along with search and rescue teams to aid distressed ships that get into trouble in these rough seas. In the various shops and bars the sailors and fisherman make their social rounds. It is a very close knit place. Now, five decades later, I understand it is something of a tourist attraction. Then it was not. On my second day in town I came across a local guy in a bar who had some very interesting stories to tell. He told me these tales after I mentioned to him that I was planning to hike up into the mountains surrounding the town for a few days of adventure. He looked at me with horror and then filled me in on what all locals knew about the surrounding mountain wilderness. Stories told in bars have a certain ring to them. It is always important to plug in how long the story teller has been sitting there drinking. My yarn spinner had just arrived so I gave his stories some credence. After hearing some of my tales he proceeded to fill me in on why they NEVER go up in the mountains. They absolutely would not go near those dangerous places after dark. I pushed him for more details on 'why not'. He looked around the room to see if any of his friends were listening and seeing no one paying him any mind, he continued on. Leaning closer to me for more privacy, he told me of the strange creatures that lurk there. He said the people of the village and these creatures had a sort of understanding; the humans would stay in the town and on the sea and the 'strange ones' would stay in the hills and mountains, especially at night. He said everyone knew of these arrangement's, even the Military and so far so good. He strongly advised me to stay away from there and especially 'them'. I bought him a drink and thanked him for the advice and left it at that.

Please let me remind you that I was in my twenties. I was in great physical condition and I had just successfully traveled over twenty five thousand miles in an old Chevy truck from the top of the world. I'd been in border shooting wars, spent time in jail, had lots of machine guns pointed at me, had run-ins with bandits, run over by a bull, been lost at sea, had nearly starved, had survived many life threating times without any weapons and now I was not going to be scared away from something I planned to do.

The next day it was cold and cloudy. It was often cold and cloudy here at the bottom of the world, I was told. I assembled my camping gear, consisting of my trusty down, mummy sleeping bag, the space blanket and some dried food I had gotten the day before. Because of all the sailors who go out to sea for days at a time, there were some very good dried fruits and edibles for sale in the little grocery store. This is the very end of the Great Cordillera de los Andes. The great mountain range that I had been following and fighting for all these many, many months; and it ended right here, diving into the violent southern sea. This is why I wanted to see them, the mountains, and say a fond fare well. I almost felt a kinship with this monster of a mountain range and I felt I might never see it again.

The climb from town was not very steep. There was no path only the peaks to aim for. It hiked gradually up a wide valley toward the snow covered high mountains. From a stand point of difficulty this was easy. This was the middle season between fall and winter. The ground was muddy and a little slippery in spots, but generally OK. After hiking for a few hours, in rugged country, I stopped to eat something. It was early afternoon but the weak sun light was already fading. I nibbled on some of the dried fruit, it was tasty and it gave me a little energy boost. The country side had no signs of human's having been there. From where I was the town could not have been but a few miles away, but no fences, no buildings, no ruins of structures even. It gave the appearance of being in a wilderness; strange being so close to civilization. It started to trouble me that no one seemed to have been here before. I convinced myself that I just wasn't seeing things correctly.

I climbed toward the high peaks, wishing to get up close and under their majesty, not actually in them. I had felt their power so many times before getting here, that I thought one more time with them hovering overhead would be a fitting 'good bye'.

The wind started to pick up and the sky looked ominous. I was in open country and not a good place to camp.

This country side is low growth bush. I'm sure in summer it's quite green, perhaps even appealing. At this time of the year it affords little to brag about. I looked about for a decent place to set up my little campsite and found one. The wind was blowing at about fifteen to twenty knots and it went right though me. I had on my down coat and two pair of pants with several long sleeved shirts but it still was cold, perhaps I was just tired of all this roughing it, I'd been doing it for a long time now. It was no time to feel sorry for myself, so I found a low bluff that gave some leeward protection from the wind and the wet weather that seemed to be coming my way. I made the classic bed out of small twigs and dead grass, put the space blanket over it and the sleeping bag on top, then made a fire. I'm not sure if there is such a thing as the ancestral memory of the open fire or not. The 'ancestral' memory is the built in or more properly 'burned in' memory of all the thousands of years our forebears sat around the fire and took comfort in the warmth and light it afforded. It likely was their only 'luxury'. When my little fire got going it was my only luxury, here in this barren landscape.

It got dark quick and the fire's glow was welcome. It's hard to keep your eyes open when there is no one to talk to and nothing but the ember's light to entertain you. The sleeping bag looks more and more like the sensible place to be. Instead of mindlessly staring at the fire you could at least disappear into your dreams with your eyes closed. Sleep in a sleeping bag is not to be compared to sound sleep in a warm soft bed. My army surplus down sleeping bag had been with me since Alaska where I bought it in an Army disposition base. This is one of the few places in America where the U.S. Military sells direct to civilians. The bag was designed for rugged wear in very cold climates and like everything the government does, it was way beyond what was needed. I loved it, it had served me well. This particular model had one extra feature. It had a little tent like roof that came up from behind your head and made a small tent over your face and chest. It kept the rain and the frost off your face. It was called a 'mummy' bag because it was caterpillar like in shape. You really put it on. There was no zipper side, just you and the fabric and the warm goose down.

I don't remember what I was dreaming about and I don't know how long I had been sleeping, likely not long, when something woke me. I'm in the middle of nowhere; no I'm at the end of nowhere, and I thought alone. You know when you are awakened from a fitful sleep you at first are not sure if you are still in your dream or awake. Something was moving behind me! Or at least around me. There was a dim glow in the western sky and I tried to use it to see what it was. I could 'see' the strange sound moving back and forth but I could not see 'IT'. I thought, maybe I'm just imagining it and I got deeper into the sleeping bag. A

little while later it seemed to get closer.
Back and forth it moved. It was a big sound.
Not the exact sound of any animal I could
identify. I had been stalked by bear in the
Yukon and recognized their sound. I had
heard many of the sounds of four legged
woodland creatures and this was not one of
them. Whatever it was; IT WAS STALKING
ME! I had survived death many times on
this journey and did want to end it here.
Maybe this is why I had continued to think
of this place as the END. No I was not going
to end it this way, but what to do. It started
to snow. This dampened some the sound of
'IT'S' movements. I still could not see it. I
could only follow it from the strange noise it
made. It was a big noise, not that of a sheep
or a dog or even a horse, but something
combining many animal sounds. Defiantly
not a friendly sound. It kept stalking. I guess
I panicked. Panic is the ability to do nothing.
Fearing for your life and thinking it is about
to end does one other thing, at least in my
case, I passed out. At least I think I did.
When daylight came I was snow covered in

my sleeping bag and still alive. I dug out, washed my face with some snow and gathered my thoughts. Was it a nightmare or was it real. I put on my boots and looked around for tracks of 'IT' and found none. Perhaps the snow had covered them. I ate some snow to clear my head further and searched the horizon for signs. Nothing visible. Was it completely my imagination or were the stories of the villagers true? Is this why they never come here.

I put a little food in my stomach and decided to call it; DONE. I got back to Ushuaia in the early afternoon and had a drink at the little bar where I had heard the stories from my sailor friend. He was there with a bunch of his friends. He called me over. I think he was surprised to see me still alive. I told the group what had happened last night. I described the sound and being stalked and the not finding any sign of the 'creature'. I asked them if they knew what it was. There was silence among the men.
They looked at each other in a knowing way and shook their heads. My sailor friend

pulled me aside and said that they hoped I had not stirred up trouble with 'IT'. I asked what was 'IT'. All he would say was, I was a lucky fellow. I was the first one to come back from there with any story to tell. Consider yourself 'lucky' and leave this place as soon as possible. He shook my hand and turned his back; I decided he was right; this was the END of it. I turned north for the first time and headed HOME!

I headed home, a mature, grown, and confident "young man" and left the naive and inexperienced "young man" that began this trip; forever in those fantastic Southern mountains.

EPILOGE

Little us, Big world

As you can imagine, I was ready to get home. Being many, many thousands of miles away, it was going to take some time. First, I had to ship the truck back to the states. Many people had offered me money for the red truck but I had a two thousand bond on it that required me to present the truck back to the Automobile Club of America in Denver to get the bond money back. Second my passport had stamped on it that I had entered Argentina with it. Customs would not let me leave the country without the proper papers showing that I had shipped it. In Buenos Aires, I found a ship going to New York, actually New Jersey, and I booked passage on it for my friend the Red truck. The day they were loading it I stood on the dock and watched as a sling was put under it and a crane on the ship hoisted it aboard with no effort. I thought of the time in Panama getting the truck on board "Good Hope". What a different experience this was. With the biggest item in my life safely on board, for the first time in a long time I only had me to worry about. I decided to go skiing. No not here in BA but in Chile at Portillo outside of the Chilean Capital, Santiago. It's easy to fly from BA to Santiago, both capital cities, only a few hours flight. Now I'm a modern guy and have flown many times. This was different. I had been sitting in the old truck for so long that the notion of airplane comfort and that I did not have to do anything and I was waited on while sitting and sitting without a steering wheel in front of me, was weird. I got used to it quickly however. When you have lived without the comforts for as long as I have, it does not take long to remember how great they are. Arriving in Santiago, a very modern airport and city, I found a small hotel for the night and inquired about skiing. I have been skiing since I was a teenager. I sort of learned on Long Island, N.Y., on a tiny slope with a rope tow. It was some of the finest ice you can get on a slope. I thought ice and slush, which occurred later in the afternoon, was what skiing was all about. I then moved to Colorado and found out ice was only in the drinks when you went skiing on real snow in the Rocky Mountains. The next day I found the bus to Portillo. This resort is not a real town but a ski resort. At least it was then. Unlike Colorado, the entire ski slope is above tree line. I don't like skiing on baron slopes. I prefer the beauty of trees and a natural wooded feel to the area. Who cares this is a treat, to be here with skis on and having a great time in a different place. I'll ski powder when I get home.

I stayed a few days in the Capitol, enjoying the Architecture and the food and people. My good old red beard let me meet a lot of people. The red beard, at a time when men did not wear them, caused people to make comments, mostly nice comments, about it and the bearer of it, me. I enjoyed myself and felt so free from all the worries I had had for so long. Life was good!

The flight to Miami was uneventful except for the fact that as we flew over some of the places I had driven all those months ago and I looked down, it was hard to believe that in a few short hours I was covering the same difficult and dangerous miles that had taken so many tough months on the road. I felt a little bit like those simple innocent people in the Alto Plano that had listened to my describing our walking on the moon. This now seemed 'other worldly'.

Miami and on to New York. I stayed at Mom's place in the city. Mom was of course delighted to see me and after the expected "why didn't you call, why didn't you write, I didn't know if you were dead;" mother required comments, she gave me a big kiss. Two weeks later the shipping company called and said the truck was at the dock in Elisabeth N.J. I got there as fast as I could, my friend was back. Lots of paper work; I can imagine what it would be like today. As the US Custom Agent took me out to the truck for the inspection, I panicked. In the big wooden box over the cab, we had stored our supply of marijuana down there in South America. We never used much of it, at least I didn't. When I shipped it from BA, in all the excitement, I forgot to clean the box out, yikes! Lucky for me it started to rain and my friendly Agent did not have on his rain coat, so he, thank goodness, made a very fast look over of the whole thing and signed off on it. Home free! Boulder Colorado here I come. Back to say good bye to Mom and on the road again.

It's almost two thousand miles from NY to Boulder. I was alone once again in the all too familiar spot behind the wheel. The familiar view through the windshield which had witnessed so many fantastic sights.

The steering wheel had my finger prints welded into it from all the white knuckle 'death roads' I had steered. How familiar it was. In those days Interstate 70 was not complete, it took longer than now. Then I was good for about 700 miles of driving without sleep. After driving for about that many miles, I took a little break in a truck stop and ate some of the sandwiches Mom had packed for me. When I started again I was still exhausted. I should have stayed one more night in NY and left fully rested, but I didn't. At the next interstate stop, I got some coffee and overheard two young guys behind me talking about their hitchhiking. I turned and asked where they were going. Denver they said. I asked if they could drive a stick shift, they both said yes. We made a deal, one would ride in the camper and one would drive, while I got some more sleep in the passenger seat. I fell asleep as soon as we left the parking lot. Unfortunately this is the only place on the entire I-70 where there is a "Y" on the interstate. Three hours later the driver woke me and said, sheepishly, "I think I made a wrong turn". Sure enough we were in Emporia Kansas, completely in the wrong place. I took the wheel and three hours later we were back at the beginning, six hours wasted. I drove the rest of the way to Denver, where they got off and forty minutes later I came over the rise to my beautiful Boulder. What a trip! Thank you for joining me.

Made in the USA
Lexington, KY
19 January 2019